GUADALUPE

Mother of the
New Creation

GUADALUPE

Mother of the
New Creation

*

VIRGIL ELIZONDO

ORBIS BOOKS

Maryknoll, New York 10545

The Catholic Foreign Mission Society of America (Maryknoll) recruits and trains people for overseas missionary service. Through Orbis Books, Maryknoll aims to foster the international dialogue that is essential to mission. The books published, however, reflect the opinions of their authors and are not meant to represent the official position of the society.

Copyright © 1997 by Virgil Elizondo
Published by Orbis Books, Maryknoll, New York, U.S.A.

Photographs courtesy of Maryknoll Archives

Manufactured in the United States of America

ISBN 1-57075-110-2

Contents

Part 1
THE POETIC MEMORY
The Creation Narrative

Part II
THE GUADALUPAN ENCOUNTER

Part III
THE NEW CREATION

Introduction

And a great sign appeared in heaven:
a woman clothed with the sun
and the moon under her feet
and upon her head, a crown of twelve stars.
And being with child,
she cried out in her travail
and was in the anguish of delivery.

—Rev. 12:1–2

Personal Story

Besides the story of Jesus of Nazareth, no other story fascinates me more than that of Our Lady of Guadalupe. She appeared to an Indian named Juan Diego in 1531 on Mount Tepeyac, on the outskirts of Mexico City. Her prodigious image and fascinating story continue to attract, console, heal, strengthen, inspire, and illuminate people throughout the Americas and beyond.

When I was six or seven, my father took me on my first pilgrimage to her shrine at Tepeyac. I will never forget it. The trip from San Antonio took three long days of difficult driving through seemingly endless deserts and then over beautiful mountains whose peaks touched the heavens. Driving in and out of the clouds was one of the most exciting adventures I had ever had. It was heavenly, and yet it was so earthy. The tropical fruit we ate on the way was the most exquisite I had ever tasted or have ever tasted since. The closer we got to Mexico City, the slower the clock seemed to move.

I had grown up hearing all kinds of marvelous stories and testimonies about Our Lady of Guadalupe. I felt I already knew her well and couldn't wait to meet her personally. The anticipation grew as we slowly walked down the Avenida de los Misterios leading to the basilica that houses her miraculous image. The long lines of vendors selling flowers, cold drinks, rosaries, tamales, medals, candles, candies, milagritos, post cards, and many other items of interest to the pilgrims added to the excitement. The praying and the singing of the people harmonized beautifully with the shouts of the vendors and the noise of the traffic. All were preparing us for the magnificent, mystical encounter that we were gradually approaching.

We finally arrived at the basilica in rhythmic procession with the thousands of others who moved, it seemed, as one collective body. When we entered through the huge doors and into the cool and dark interior (it was very hot outside), it was as if we were all entering together into the common womb of the Americas. As we gradually walked toward the luminous image, she appeared to be coming toward us, as if she were descending to greet each one of us personally. Through the darkness we walked toward the light, the warmth, and the beauty of La Virgen Morena. We could not stop; the crowd simply moved us on. We were never pushed or shoved; we all simply walked in deep mystical union with one another. We were in the rhythmic movement of the universe — indeed, at this moment we were in contact with the very source of life and movement.

I needed no explanation for my experience. I had lived it. In that sacred space, I was part of the communion of earth and heaven, of present family, ancestors, and generations to come. It became one of the core moments of my life. Returning many years later to celebrate one of my first masses at the altar beneath her image was an equally special moment of my life. And when I went there in September of 1995 to finish these meditations, I was once again fascinated by what I saw and experienced. She is always there — for me and for all others.

The more I meditate on the story, contemplate the image, and reflect on the impact of the Guadalupe event on people, society, and the church, the more I realize how extraordinary it was and continues to be. Its full impact can be appreciated only in the context of salvation history itself. For Guadalupe is not just a Mexican happening — it is a major moment in God's saving plan for humanity.

The more I try to comprehend the intrinsic force and energy of the apparitions of Our Lady of Guadalupe to Juan Diego in Tepeyac in 1531, at the very beginning of the Americas, the more I dare to say that I do not know of any other event since Pentecost that has had such a revolutionary, profound, lasting, far-reaching, healing, and liberating impact on Christianity. The evolution of my own appreciation of Guadalupe has progressed gradually and continues to become more exciting and enriching. It started early in my life as a warm neighborhood devotion that saw Guadalupe as a very Mexican manifestation of the Virgin Mary. In time, I started to recognize her as the foundation of Mexican identity and Mexican Catholicism. Growing up in the southwestern United States, I realized that it was her devotees, the Guadalupana societies, that had kept our people Catholic even when we had not had the services of priests and religious.

As I started to explore her theological significance, I began to see her as the great evangelizer of the church and of the Americas and then as the protector and liberator of the poor, the downtrodden, and the disenfranchised. This gave rise to my book *La Morenita: Evangelizer of the Americas* and to subsequent articles in *Concilium*. Today, I see her as the beginning of a new creation, the mother of a new humanity, and the manifestation of the femininity of God — a figure offering unlimited possibilities for creative and liberating reflection. Juan Diego is the prototype of the new human being of the Americas. I see the story of her encounters with Juan Diego, of Juan Diego's encounters with the bishop, and of the healing of Juan Diego's uncle, Juan Bernardino, being as miraculous as the image itself.

Some may have doubts about the exact origins of this tradition, but no one can deny her presence on the *tilma* and, even more than that, her living presence in the growing number of her followers across the Americas and beyond. Through songs, poems, artworks, plays, personal testimonies of favors granted, and the religious imagination of the people, her presence continues to grow and expand far beyond the confines of any church or organized movement.

Her presence in the consciousness of the people makes her present today, as that consciousness continues to re-create and transmit her loving, compassionate, and healing presence and message to new places around the globe and to future generations. Our Lady of Guadalupe is not a dogma of Christian faith, but she is definitely among the most tender, beautiful, vibrant, and influential truths of the Christianity of the Americas.

Even if the story of Our Lady of Guadalupe were not historical (according to modern Western historiography), it is still definitely constitutive of the saving truth of the *sensus fidelium* — of the faith-memory of the people. The story, like the image, is so packed with the word of life expressed in human terms, is so beautiful and harmonious, is so critical and melodious, is so theological and poetic, is so simple and profound, and is so affirming and challenging that it can only be a very special gift of the creating and redeeming God.

I do not believe that my explanations will prove anything about the apparitions or increase the devotion, which will continue with or without explanations, but I do hope that they can help those who believe in Our Lady of Guadalupe to deepen their appreciation of the transforming, liberating, and life-giving role that she had in history and continues to have today. The starting point for my interest is not only my own personal devotion to her but also the increasing devotion of the masses of the people of the Americas. What could give Guadalupe such unquestioned credibility? such power? such faithful followers? such an exalted position? such universal recognition?

I will begin by trying to see, hear, and understand what the Guadalupe event meant in its origins and will then proceed to reflect on its greater meaning for the church and society. Guadalupe is definitely a very popular devotion, but behind this devotion lie also a new image and understanding of reality, of truth, of humanity, and of God. Guadalupe will give the world a new way of relating religions and peoples to each other: no longer by way of opposition but by way of synthesis, for even the most contradictory forces can be brought together creatively for the sake of a truly new humanity.

The Uniqueness of the Historical Moment

The story of Our Lady of Guadalupe really begins in 1492: one of the most fascinating years in all of history. The last crusade had come to an end with the battle of Granada on January 2, 1492. Christian Spain was euphoric over the military triumph of the Christians over the Moors. The Christian empire, radiating from the Catholic monarchs of Spain, now felt a divine mandate to expand to the rest of the non-Christian world for the greater honor and glory of God. Wealth, power, and eternal salvation would henceforth become the motivating forces for the new enterprises to come. New lands with apparently unlimited resources — especially land, gold, and the imagined fountain of youth — would emerge to excite the adventuresome and conquering spirit of the Europeans. For Europe, it was the beginning of totally new opportunities for fame, wealth, and adventure. For the church, it was the opportunity to build a new church that could be truly evangelical, a church that would not be contaminated by the many abuses that had ruined the old church of Europe and in many ways distanced it from the gospel.[1]

For the natives of the Americas, 1492 was quite the opposite. It was the beginning of the invasion of gun-bearing gods-turned-monsters from unknown lands against whom their own weapons and tactics of war seemed totally impotent. That year was the beginning of their condemnation to hard labor, humiliation, destruction, sickness, enslavement, and massive death.[2]

---

1. This was the great dream and vision of the early missioners to the Americas — to build an Indian church that would not be contaminated with the perverted church of Europe. There are many good works on this topic, among them: Ed Sylvest, *Motifs of Franciscan Missionary Spirit in New Spain* (Washington, D.C.: Academy of American Franciscan History, 1975); Jacques Lafaye, *Quetzalcoatl and Guadalupe* (Chicago: University of Chicago Press, 1976); and Richard Nebel, *Santa María Tonantzin: Virgen de Guadalupe* (Mexico City: Fondo de Cultura Económica, 1995).

2. For a very good summary yet in-depth study of the implications of this invasion and the unequal encounters of the various peoples of the globe, see Leonardo Boff and Virgil Elizondo, eds., *1492–1992: The Voice of the Victims*, vol. 1990/6 of *Concilium* (London: SCM Press, 1990). See also Casiano Floristán, "Evangelization of the 'New World': An Old World Perspective," *Missiology* 20, no. 2 (1992): 133–49.

Along with the cruel monsters came new "priests" — ambiguous figures who seemed different from the monsters yet still eager to destroy them, though in a different way. Some of these priests lived among the natives, learned their languages and customs, were concerned for their welfare, cared for them, and tried to befriend them. Nevertheless, they sought to destroy that which was most sacred to the natives: the religious traditions of their ancestors. Without these, the natives' world would have no meaning or value; only chaos and emptiness would reign. Thus for the natives, the kindness of the missioners covered a deeper violence and a more subtle form of cruelty — definitely not intended as such, but, tragically, that is the way it functioned. Henceforth, the natives would permanently be aliens in their own lands — deprived of everything, including their own priests. The year 1492 marks the beginning of the hurricane that continues to be so destructive of the native life — natural and human — of the Americas.

It is next to impossible for us today to understand or appreciate the far-reaching impact of the events and processes that were unleashed with the first coming together of Europeans and Amerindians. Two groups that had never suspected the existence of each other suddenly found themselves face-to-face, and in that moment the horizons of both expanded almost infinitely. Each had been developing in very different ways. Each civilization had produced languages, philosophies, great artistic works, sophisticated crafts, and complex religions. Each had its unique ways of approaching truth, expressing beauty, and communicating with ultimate reality. Each was guided by different value systems, different systems of logic, different anthropologies, and different mythologies. Europeans had known of the great, mysterious differences between themselves and the peoples of some other great continents, but they had not even suspected the existence of the continent they ran into beginning in 1492. Here they encountered not only an unsuspected continent but a different humanity, that is, a people with a cosmovision totally different from their own. In great awe, each asked: Who are these strange people? Are they human? Are they devils?

For the Europeans, the true, good, and beautiful human being was a rational individual who could conquer whatever he or she set out to obtain and control. According to this view, anyone who did not seek to conquer was an inferior and weak human being who should be dominated by the "superior" peoples of the earth. In contrast, the indigenous world of knowledge saw the human as a creature whose very existence depended on interconnectedness within the self, nation, earth, creation, and beyond. Two anthropologies clashed: the European anthropology of rationality and the native anthropology of creatureliness.[3] For the Europeans, conquest — of self and of others — was the measure of the human, while for the Amerindians, harmony within the self and all of creation was the measure of the human. The former view emphasized argumentation and linear discourse; the latter view emphasized cosmic signs and rituals. One was a world of reason, logic, and argumentation while the other was a world of omens, dreams, myths, and rituals. One was obsessed with the spirit of conquest — physical and/or spiritual — while the other was obsessed with a spirit of radical acceptance of the cosmic order as it was.[4]

Despite their great accomplishments and achievements, each of the civilizations had ended up immersed in a type of horrible violence that appeared logical and even necessary to itself but totally incomprehensible to the other. Partial anthropologies always end up in violence. In effect, neither was complete without the other; each needed the other so as to become fully human. Both were as fascinated with each other as they were frightened of each other.

The Europeans marveled at the incredible order and beauty of the great imperial city of Tenochtitlán (Mexico City), while they were horrified and scandalized by the human sacrifices that took place there. The Amerindians marveled at the men on horseback who had arrived on huge moving islands and had the magic weapons that could destroy at a distance, but they were horrified by their cruelty and the ease with which they killed men, women, and

---

3. For an excellent analysis of these two anthropologies, see Alejandro García-Rivera, *St. Martin de Porres: The "Little Stories" and the Semiotics of Culture* (Maryknoll, N.Y.: Orbis Books, 1995).

4. See J. M. G. Le Clezio, *The Mexican Dream: The Interrupted Thought of Amerindian Civilizations* (Chicago: University of Chicago Press, 1993).

innocent children in senseless massacres. The violence of each was a scandal for the other and made any real dialogue and personal interchange impossible.

The horrible and the beautiful of both worlds had now come together in a new struggle, one that would be unequal in one very important aspect: the Europeans had a definite superiority in the instruments and techniques of war. In addition, their bodies had naturally developed immunity to the diseases that they carried with them into the New World and that the bodies of the natives were totally unprepared for. Between war and new diseases, the native population would come close to being annihilated. The struggle for life and survival would definitely not be on equal terms.

The unity of two vast segments of the human race was now physically possible, but instead, their contact marked the beginning of the present-day structures of world domination, segregation, margination, and enslavement. The structures of the physical and spiritual oppression of the natives, their mestizo children, the Africans forced into slavery, and the slaves' children would become so entrenched that five hundred years later they seem to be impossible to overcome. Henceforth, the world would be racially and religiously divided by barriers that seemed impenetrable. An abyss was created that to this day appears impossible to bridge. The source of this great tragedy was that the white Europeans saw themselves as having absolute dominion over all the non-Christian lands of the globe, as being the only civilized human beings and the exclusive possessors of all truth. Their arrogance in all matters relating to human and divine life would be legitimized not by the inner strength of truth but by the technological power that they developed and that made it possible for them to impose their worldview upon everyone else.

With the end of the crusades, the old ideal of the universal Christian empire had fueled, legitimized, and given a religious justification to the new conquests.[5] In the name and for the sake of Christ, the world had to be conquered and brought under his do-

---

5. Luis N. Rivera Pagán, *A Violent Evangelization* (Louisville: Westminster/John Knox Press, 1992).

main, which on earth meant under the domain of the pope and the king and queen of Spain. Whatever was not in accordance with the imagery and ways of the Euro-Christian worldview, especially in matters of religion, had to be destroyed. The Europeans came with a preconceived horror of anything linked to other religions and proceeded with a fanatic zeal to destroy as diabolical everything of the indigenous religions, which meant the brutal destruction of the deepest roots of Indian existence and the collective soul of the native peoples. This mentality would constrain and poison the missioners and keep them from entering into any type of real dialogue with the native peoples while at the same time deepening the collective trauma of the conquest.[6]

To those who lived these moments of history, it was evident that they were experiencing an event of planetary magnitude. It is no wonder that in 1552, Francisco López de Gomara, an eyewitness of that event, described it in these terms: "The greatest thing after the creation of the world, except for the incarnation and death of the one who created it, is the discovery of the Indies, the so-called New-World."[7] For Bartolomé de las Casas, in spite of the cruelties and abuses of the conquest, which he condemned vigorously and without hesitation, this moment was "the time of the merciful marvels of God" in which Christ's commandment to evangelize the whole world could now be fulfilled.[8] It was truly a historical *kairós*, the foundation of an eschatological *oikouméne*. And Pope Alexander VI would give praise to God because God had opened a "path for the beginning of the ultimate preaching of the Gospel and convocation,...the eleventh hour of human history." For the pope of that period, these events had a deep, universal significance in God's plan. They were the beginning of the final days of humanity.[9]

For the first time, all humanity had the possibility of being

---

6. Miguel León-Portilla, *Endangered Cultures* (Dallas: Southern Methodist University Press, 1990); Floristán, "Evangelization of the 'New World': An Old World Perspective," 143.

7. Cited in Luis N. Rivera Pagán, "Conquest and Colonization: The Problem of America," *Apuntes* 12, no. 2 (1992): 44.

8. Rivera Pagán, *A Violent Evangelization*, 58–59.

9. Rivera Pagán, "Conquest and Colonization," 44–46.

united together as brothers and sisters under the parenthood of the one God who is father and mother of all. It was an incredible opportunity and challenge. And it was a tragedy that such an opportunity of grace became one of the most painful and scandalous chapters of history.

The Voice of the Silenced

Gomara and the others assessed the planetary significance of these events correctly, but the real and ultimate newness of the events would be revealed in ways that none of them suspected. As the savior of the world entered the world not through the Pax Romana of the Roman Empire but through the birth of a powerless and defenseless baby in Bethlehem, so would the real new world — the new humanity of the Americas, the beginning of a new creation — begin with the marvelous and unsuspected eruption that God would bring about at Tepeyac through the mediation of Juan Diego in 1531.

The story of Our Lady of Guadalupe is the indigenous account of the real new beginnings of the Americas. The story of her appearances and compassion is sacred narrative as remembered by the victim-survivors of the conquest who were equally the firstborn of the new creation. The entire Guadalupe event as recorded in the *Nican Mopohua* is a Nahuatl communication par excellence. It proceeds by way of contrasting images whose full meaning is arrived at only in the final synthesis. The symbolic meaning of the images created by the words is all-important. Each detail had special signification for the Nahuatl peoples. The story came from their world, and if we are to discover its regenerative signification, we must seek to understand it through their cosmovision.

The whole Guadalupe narrative is a beautiful, delicate, and carefully thought-out Nahuatl poem of contrasting imagery, symbolic communication, tender consolation, radical affirmation, and divine inversion. It is a highly complex mestizo (Nahuatl-European) form of communication in various ways: the image and the narrative are mutually interpretative; there are elements of both Nahuatl and

Iberian worldviews in the narrative and the image, and together they say new things that neither alone could have expressed; the image is poetry that is seen while the poem is imagery that is heard, and together they constitute a coherent communication.

While the sacred imagery of the native world was being insulted, discredited, and burned, the sacred imagery of the Christian world was being imposed as the sole representation of that which was good, beautiful, and true. This did not make sense to peoples whose sacred imagery had guided their lives from time immemorial. Furthermore, it was alien to the gospel itself. But now, a new Nahuatl-Christian sacred imagery would erupt from within these tensions.

The full life-giving meaning of Guadalupe can be seen and understood only in the overall context of the confused and painful reality of the postconquest period. The Aztec-Nahuatl Empire, and with it all the native peoples, was defeated in 1531. It was the beginning of the end of their world. Their entire world of meaning had been destroyed and discredited. Had their ancestors been wrong all along and therefore to be disclaimed? Were they now to be ashamed of their parents and ancestors? Were they now to cut off all family tradition and relations? Had their God deceived them for generations? Since the conquering people, who claimed their European God was all-powerful, were white men and women, did that mean that their brown skin was an indication of their inferiority or even of their collective sinful condition? Would grace make them white with blue eyes?

It seemed the sun had been permanently eclipsed, and the innermost darkness of the soul prevailed throughout the land and its native peoples. In the midst of the death cries of a vanquished people, a new light broke through to announce new life. This was the good news of Our Lady of Guadalupe — the gospel through the language and imagery of the conquered people of the Nahuatl world.

The gospel through Our Lady of Guadalupe has been kept alive, interiorized, assimilated, and transmitted by the Spirit through song and dance. The deep joy that the Guadalupe experience brought about was spontaneously communicated like wildfire —

first among the conquered Indians and then in time to the mestizo and creole society. Like the Gospel stories of Jesus, the Guadalupe narrative is so simple that no one at first imagined that it was a new chapter in the long and mysterious journey of the religious encounters of the planet. After the events at Guadalupe, the Indians danced on the feast of December 12, singing in Nahuatl how the Virgin appeared to Juan Diego, healed his uncle, and painted herself on Juan Diego's *tilma* in the presence of the bishop.[10] At their core, these elements harmonize with the basic elements of the earliest kerygma, and like the earliest preaching of the apostles (who simply stated: you killed him, but God has raised him from the dead), the Guadalupan proclamation is simple but profound. And just as the New Testament emerged through the singing of inspired songs of the primitive Christian community, so the narrative of Guadalupe emerged through song and dance.

In the context of the dances, the *mitotes* (native socioreligious festivals) that the missioners had abhorred, the Indians expressed themselves in great freedom, dancing with great fervor and singing with great joy. In these moments, they were free to be who they truly were and to enter into communion with the world of the divine in ways that truly made sense to them. It was the Nahuatl proclamation of the Easter joy. It was as if they were saying: "They tried to kill us, but God has raised us to life. They tried to destroy the ways of life of our ancestors, but God has protected us and redeemed us."

The joy of Easter, the new dawn of the early morning sunrise, comes only after the long day of absolute silence and darkness while the crucified victim remains in the tomb. It is the day of desolation and absolute darkness. Our Guadalupe poem begins with the darkness of death and will lead us to the joyful brightness of the new day.

---

10. Clodomiro L. Siller Acuña, *Para comprender el mensaje de María de Guadalupe* (Buenos Aires: Editorial Guadalupe, 1989), 12.

Part 1

THE POETIC MEMORY
The Creation Narrative

* *
*

Introduction to
the Nican Mopohua

The *Nican Mopohua* is a careful and serious attempt to put in writing the memory of the prodigious events of 1531.[1] It was written by a Nahuatl scholar, in Nahuatl, for the Nahuatl people. Its complex and inexact origins are quite problematic (as are those of the Gospels) for modern historians who have created criteria of history that were not necessarily those of the times of the *Nican Mopohua* (or of the Gospels). Nevertheless, like the Gospels, the force of this text lies not in its exact historical origins but in the fact that it has been consistently re-created in its faithful retelling by those for whom it has ultimate meaning. Regardless of its historical origins, nobody can deny that it is very alive today.

Don Angel María Garibay, one of the greatest historians of Mexico and of the Guadalupe events, states that this Nahuatl poem is one of great harmony and depth. It is a masterpiece of Nahuatl literature. The language of the poem gives great emphasis to visual precision, elegance, beauty, sound, and symbolic meaning. Hence every detail and the way the details relate to one another are important to the communication. The language embodies the entire Nahuatl cosmovision, which was totally different from that of the Europeans.

To understand and appreciate the poem, every attempt must be made not just to read it but to experience it with all the senses, the mind, and the heart. For example, the word (and image) "flower"

---

1. For a full description of the origins and development of the *Nican Mopohua*, see Clodomiro L. Siller Acuña, *Para comprender el mensaje de María de Guadalupe* (Buenos Aires: Editorial Guadalupe, 1989), 11–16, and Richard Nebel, *Santa María Tonantzin: Virgen de Guadalupe* (Mexico City: Fondo de Cultura Económica, 1995), 167–264.

3

signifies truth while "beauty" signifies authenticity and philosophy. Just as we try to understand the Scriptures in their original context and meaning, so must we try to understand the *Nican Mopohua* in its original context.

I present here my own translation from the Spanish of Clodomiro L. Siller Acuña. The latter is a translation from the Nahuatl originally written by Don Antonio Valeriano of the Colegio de la Santa Cruz of Tlatelolco and coming to us through the work of Garibay. Of the various Spanish translations available, I have found Siller Acuña's to be the best. The present book relies heavily not only on his excellent text of the poem but also on his superb commentary.[2]

---

2. See Siller Acuña, *Para comprender el mensaje de María de Guadalupe.*

The Text of
the Nican Mopohua

✳ Title ✳

[1] Here we recount in an orderly way how the Ever-Virgin Holy Mary, Mother of God, our Queen, appeared recently in a marvelous way at Tepeyac, which is called Guadalupe.[1]

✳ Summary ✳

[2] First she allowed herself to be seen by a poor and dignified person whose name is Juan Diego; and then her precious image appeared in the presence of the new bishop D. Fray Juan de Zumárraga. The many marvels that she has brought about are also told.

✳ The Situation of the City and Its Inhabitants ✳

[3] Ten years after the conquest of the city of Mexico, arrows and shields were put down; everywhere the inhabitants of the lake and the mountain had surrendered.

---

1. Tepeyac was the sacred mountain site of the goddess Tonantzin, where she had been venerated from time immemorial. Gradually it came to be known as Guadalupe. Why it came to be known as Guadalupe (from Our Lady of Guadalupe in Extremadura in Spain) is not known, but it was certainly known by that name by 1575. Gradually Our Lady became known by that name. In the redaction of the *Nican Mopohua,* the origins of the designation are attributed to Juan Bernardino.

5

[4] Thus faith started; it gave its first buds; and it flowered in the knowledge of the One through Whom We Live, the true God, Téotl.[2]

[5] Precisely in the year 1531, a few days after the beginning of December, a poor, dignified campesino was in the surroundings [of Tepeyac]. His name was Juan Diego. It was said that his home was in Cuauhtitlán.[3]

[6] And insofar as the things of God, all that region belonged to Tlatelolco.[4]

✳ First Encounter with the Virgin ✳

[7] It was Saturday, when it was still night. He was going in search of the things of God and of God's messages. [8] And when he arrived at the side of the small hill, which was named Tepeyac, it was already beginning to dawn.

[9] He heard singing on the summit of the hill: as if different precious birds were singing and their songs would alternate, as if the hill was answering them. Their song was most pleasing and very enjoyable, better than that of the coyoltotl or of the tzinizcan or of the other precious birds that sing.[5]

[10] Juan Diego stopped and said to himself: "By chance do I deserve this? Am I worthy of what I am hearing? Maybe I am dreaming? Maybe I only see this in my dreams? Where am I? [11] Maybe I am in the land of my ancestors, of the elders, of our

---

2. "Téotl" was the designation for the God of the Nahuatls while "true God" was the designation for the God of the Christian Spaniards. In using the phrase "true God, Téotl," the text is thus linking the God of the Nahuatls and the God of the Christians.

3. The use of the word "Cuauhtitlán" indicates that Juan Diego was from the place of the eagles, which was symbolic of the sun; it indicates he was from the land of the people of the sun. By saying he was from there, the text is pointing out that he would be explaining the things of God (see Siller Acuña, *Para comprender el mensaje*, 60).

4. This was an ancient ceremonial center that had become a center of Spanish evangelization and spiritual domination (see Siller Acuña, *Para comprender el mensaje*, 60).

5. Birds in Nahuatl thought indicate mediation between heaven and earth; the coyoltotl was the symbol of great fecundity.

grandparents? In the Land of Flower, in the Earth of our flesh? Maybe over there inside of heaven?"

[12] His gaze was fixed on the summit of the hill, toward the direction from which the sun arises: the beautiful celestial song was coming from there to here. [13] And when the song finally ceased, when everything was calm, he heard that he was being called from the summit of the hill. He heard: "Dignified Juan, dignified Juan Diego."

[14] Then he dared to go to where he was being called. His heart was in no way disturbed, and in no way did he experience any fear; on the contrary, he felt very good, very happy.

[15] He went to the top of the hill, and he saw a lady who was standing and who was calling him to come closer to her side. [16] When he arrived in her presence, he marveled at her perfect beauty. [17] Her clothing appeared like the sun, and it gave forth rays.

[18] And the rock and the cliffs where she was standing, upon receiving the rays like arrows of light, appeared like precious emeralds, appeared like jewels; the earth glowed with the splendors of the rainbow. The mesquites, the cacti, and the weeds that were all around appeared like feathers of the quetzal, and the stems looked like turquoise; the branches, the foliage, and even the thorns sparkled like gold.

[19] He bowed before her, heard her thought and word, which were exceedingly re-creative, very ennobling, alluring, producing love. [20] She said: "Listen, my most abandoned son, dignified Juan: Where are you going?"

[21] And he answered: "My Owner and my Queen: I have to go to your house of Mexico-Tlatelolco, to follow the divine things that our priests, who are the images of our Lord, give to us." [22] Then she conversed with him and unveiled her precious will. She said: "Know and be certain in your heart,[6] my most abandoned son, that I am the Ever-Virgin Holy Mary, Mother of the God of Great Truth, Téotl, of the One through Whom We Live, the Cre-

---

6. The heart is the active and dynamic center of the person; it is the symbolic place of ultimate understanding and certitude. Truth resides in the heart.

ator of Persons, the Owner of What Is Near and Together, of the Lord of Heaven and Earth.[7]

[23] "I very much want and ardently desire that my hermitage[8] be erected in this place. In it I will show and give to all people all my love, my compassion, my help, and my protection, [24] because I am your merciful mother and the mother of all the nations that live on this earth who would love me, who would speak with me, who would search for me, and who would place their confidence in me. [25] There I will hear their laments and remedy and cure all their miseries, misfortunes, and sorrows.

[26] "And for this merciful wish of mine to be realized, go there to the palace of the bishop of Mexico, and you will tell him in what way I have sent you as messenger, so that you may make known to him how I very much desire that he build me a home right here, that he may erect my temple[9] on the plain. You will tell him carefully everything you have seen and admired and heard.

[27] "Be absolutely certain that I will be grateful and will repay you; and because of this I will make you joyful; I will give you happiness; and you will earn much that will repay you for your trouble and your work in carrying out what I have entrusted to you. Look, my son the most abandoned one, you have heard my statement and my word; now do everything that relates to you."

[28] Then he bowed before her and said to her: "My Owner and my Queen, I am already on the way to make your statement and your word a reality. And now I depart from you, I your poor servant." Then he went down so as to make her commission a reality; he went straight to the road that leads directly to Mexico [City].

---

7. This litany of names is a most important revelation, for they are the same names that were mentioned by the Nahuatl theologians in their dialogues with the Spanish theologians and that were discredited by the Spanish evangelizers. They appeared in the purest preconquest theology of the Nahuatls. She reestablishes the authenticity and veracity of these holy names. The names refer to neither demons nor false idols; they are venerable names of God.

8. "Hermitage" could refer to a home for the homeless, an orphanage, a hospice — all would have a special meaning for a people who had been totally displaced and left homeless by the conquest.

9. Notice the progression from hermitage (home for the homeless), to a home (place of affectionate relationships), to a temple (the manifestation of the sacred). Thus, where everyone is welcomed *is* sacred earth.

✳ First Interview with the Bishop ✳

[29] Having entered the city, he went directly to the palace of
the bishop, who had recently arrived as the lord of the priests; his
name was Don Fray Juan de Zumárraga, a priest of Saint Francis.

[30] As soon as he [Juan Diego] arrived, he tried to see him [the
lord bishop]. He begged his servants, his attendants, to go speak to
him. After a long time, they came to call him, telling him that the
lord bishop had ordered him to come in. As soon as he entered, he
prostrated himself and then knelt. [31] Immediately he presented,
he revealed, the thought and the word of the Lady from Heaven
and her will. And he also told him everything he had admired, seen,
and heard. When he [the bishop] heard all his words, his message,
it was as if he didn't give it much credibility. [32] He answered him
and told him: "My son, you will have to come another time; I will
calmly listen to you at another time. I still have to see, to examine
carefully from the very beginning, the reason you have come, and
your will and your wish."

[33] He left very saddened because in no way whatsoever had
her message been accomplished.

✳ Second Encounter with the Virgin ✳

[34] The same day, he returned [to Tepeyac]. He came to the
summit of the hill and found the Lady from Heaven: she was
waiting in the very same spot where he had seen her the first time.

[35] When he saw her, he prostrated himself before her, he fell
upon the earth and said: "My Owner, my Matron, my Lady, the
most abandoned of my Daughters, my Child, I went where you
sent me to deliver your thought and your word. [36] With great
difficulty I entered the place of the lord of the priests; I saw him;
before him I expressed your thought and word, just as you had
ordered me. [37] He received me well and listened carefully. But
by the way he answered me, as if his heart had not accepted it, [I
know] he did not believe it. He told me: 'You will have to come
another time; I will calmly listen to you at another time. I still have

to see, to examine carefully from the very beginning, the reason you have come, and your will and your wish.' [38] I saw perfectly, in the way he answered me, that he thinks that possibly I am just making it up that you want a temple to be built on this site, and possibly it is not your command.¹⁰

[39] "Hence, I very much beg you, my Owner, my Queen, my Child, that you charge one of the more valuable nobles, a well-known person, one who is respected and esteemed, to come by and take your message and your word so that he may be believed. [40] Because in reality I am one of those campesinos, a piece of rope,¹¹ a small ladder,¹² the excrement of people; I am a leaf;¹³ they order me around, lead me by force;¹⁴ and you, my most abandoned Daughter, my Child, my Lady, and my Queen, send me to a place where I do not belong.¹⁵ [41] Forgive me, I will cause pain to your countenance and to your heart; I will displease you and fall under your wrath, my Lady and my Owner."¹⁶

[42] The ever-venerated Virgin answered: "Listen, my most abandoned son, know well in your heart that there are not a few of my servants and messengers to whom I could give the mandate of taking my thought and my word so that my will may be accomplished. But it is absolutely necessary that you personally go and speak about this, and that precisely through your mediation and help, my wish and my desire be realized.¹⁷ [43] I beg you very

---

10. In the presence of those in power, the poor understand very well that they are not credible.

11. The reference is to the rope that was tied around the Indians' necks as they were chained and pulled around for forced labor.

12. The Indians were "stepped on" in the process by which others climbed the ladder of social and economic mobility. They were often used as beasts of burden.

13. Dried leaves were used to wipe oneself after a bowel movement.

14. The worst part of domination is that the oppressed begin to believe what those in authority say: that they are subhuman, inferior, incapable of dignified tasks, and a burden to society.

15. The text literally says "a place where I do not walk or put my foot upon." This is the Nahuatl expression for a place where one does not belong, that is, a place where one is not wanted or allowed in.

16. This is a perfect example of the soul-crushing victimization of the victims of society: They are made to feel guilty for their situation of misery and deserving of disgust and punishment.

17. Consistent with the Gospels and the beginnings of the apostolic movement, it is precisely through the mediation of the "nothings of this world" (1 Corinthi-

much, my most abandoned son, and with all my energy I command that precisely tomorrow you go again to see the bishop. [44] In my name you will make him know, make him listen well to my wish and desire, so that he may make my wish a reality and build my temple. And tell him once again that I personally, the Ever-Virgin Mary, the Mother of the God Téotl, am the one who is sending you there."

[45] Juan Diego answered her: "My Owner, my Lady, my Child, I will not cause pain to your countenance and your heart. With a very good disposition of my heart, I will go; there I will go to tell him truthfully your thought and your word. In no way whatsoever will I fail to do it; it will not be painful for me to go. [46] I will go to do your will. But it could well be that I will not be listened to; and if I am listened to, possibly I will not be believed. [47] Tomorrow in the afternoon, when the sun sets,[18] I will return your thought and word to you, what the lord of the priests [has] answer[ed] me.

[48] "Now I take leave of you, my most abandoned Daughter, my Child, my Matron, my Lady, now you rest a bit." Then he went to his home to rest.

✳ Second Interview with the Bishop ✳

[49] The next day, Sunday, when it was still night, when it was still dark, he left his home and went directly to Tlatelolco to learn about the things divine, and to answer roll call so that afterward he could see the lord of the priests.

---

ans 1:28), through the "stone rejected by the builders of this world" (Acts 4:11), that the reign of God will erupt into this world. In the *Nican Mopohua*, the home-temple that the Lady requests is equivalent to the "kingdom" in the Gospel stories. It will begin through the mediation of the poor and the lowly of this world, to whom the kingdom belongs (see *Catechism of the Catholic Church*, no. 544). It is they who will invite all others into the new family home for God's children. The abandoned of this world act under the authority of God.

18. "In the afternoon, when the sun sets," is the Nahuatl expression for coming to an end of a period of life and the expectation of something new that is about to begin. It is an expression of hope. Here it could easily mean, "Tomorrow, hoping that something new will take place..."

[50] Around ten in the morning, when they had gathered together and heard mass and answered roll call and the poor had been dispersed, Juan Diego went immediately to the house of the lord bishop.

[51] And when he arrived there, he made every effort to see him, and with great difficulty he succeeded in seeing him. He knelt at his feet; he cried and became very sad as he was communicating and unveiling before him the thought and the word of the Lady from Heaven, hoping to be accepted as her messenger and believing that it was the will of the Ever Virgin to have him build a dwelling in the place where she wanted it.

[52] But the lord bishop asked him many questions; he interrogated him as to where he saw her and all about her so as to satisfy his heart. And he told the lord bishop everything.

[53] But even though he told him everything, all about her figure, all that he had seen and admired, and how she had shown herself to be the lovable Ever Virgin and admirable mother of our Lord and our Savior Jesus Christ,[19] yet, he still did not believe him.

[54] He [the bishop] told him that he could not proceed on her wishes just on the basis of his word and message. A sign from her would be necessary for the bishop to believe that he [Juan Diego] was indeed sent by the Lady from Heaven. [55] When Juan Diego heard this, he told the bishop: "My patron and my lord, what is the sign that you want? [When I know, I can] go and ask the Lady from Heaven, she who sent me here." The bishop was impressed that he was so firm in the truth, that he did not doubt anything or hesitate in any way. He dismissed him.

[56] And when he had left, he [the lord bishop] sent some people from his household in whom he trusted, to follow him and observe where he went, what he saw, and with whom he was speaking. And so it was done. [57] And Juan Diego went directly down the road.

---

19. Note that it is Juan Diego who recognizes her as the mother of Jesus Christ. She never mentions this in her conversations with him. It is he who makes the connection and thus announces to his people that the mother of their Nahuatl God "Téotl" and the mother of the Spanish God "Dios" is likewise the mother of the one and only savior of all, Jesus Christ.

His followers took the same route. Close to the bridge of Tepeyac, in the hillside, they lost sight of him; they kept looking for him everywhere, but they could not find him anyplace.

[58] Thus they returned infuriated and were angered at him because he frustrated their intentions. [59] In this state of mind, they went to inform the lord bishop, creating in him a bad attitude so that he would not believe him; they told him that he was only deceiving him; that he was only imagining what he was coming to say; that he was only dreaming; or that he had invented what he was coming to tell him. They agreed among themselves that if he were to come again, they would grab him and punish him harshly, so that he would not lie again or deceive the people.

＊ Juan Diego Takes Care of His Uncle ＊

[60] On the next day, Monday, when Juan Diego was supposed to take something to be the sign by which he was to be believed, he did not return, because when he arrived home, one of his uncles, named Juan Bernardino, had caught the smallpox and was in his last moments.

[61] First he went to call a doctor, who helped him, but he could do no more because he [Juan Bernardino] was already gravely ill. [62] Through the night, his uncle begged him that while it was still dark, he should go to Tlatelolco to call a priest to come and hear his confession and prepare him well because he felt deeply in his heart that this was the time and place of his death, that he would not be healed.

＊ Third Encounter with the Virgin ＊

[63] And on Tuesday, when it was still night, Juan Diego left his home to go to Tlatelolco to call a priest.

[64] And when he arrived at the side of Mount Tepeyac at the point where the road leads out, on the side on which the sun sets, the side he was accustomed to take, he said: [65] "If I take this

road, it is quite possible that the Lady will come to see me as before and will hold me back so that I may take the sign to the lord of the priests as she had instructed me. [66] But first I must attend to our affliction and quickly call the priest. My uncle is agonizing and is waiting for him."

[67] He then went around the hill; he climbed through the middle; and he went to the other side, to the side of the sunrise, so as to arrive quickly into Mexico, and to avoid the Lady from Heaven delaying him. [68] He thought that having taken this other route, he would not be seen by the one who cares for everyone.

[69] He saw her coming down from the top of the hill; and from there, where he had seen her before, she had been watching him. She came to him at the side of the hill, blocked his passage, and, standing in front of him, said: "My most abandoned son, where are you going? In what direction are you going?"

[70] Did he become embarrassed a bit? Was he ashamed? Did he feel like running away? Was he fearful? He bowed before her, greeted her, and said: "My Child, my most abandoned Daughter, my Lady, I hope you are happy. How did the dawn come upon you? Does your body feel all right, my Owner and my Child? [71] I am going to give great pain to your countenance and heart. You must know, my Child, that my uncle, a poor servant of yours, is in his final agony; a great illness has fallen upon him, and because of it he will die.

[72] I am in a hurry to get to your house in Mexico; I am going to call one of the beloved of our Lord, one of our priests, so that he may go and hear his confession and prepare him. [73] Because for this have we been born, to await the moment of our death. [74] But if right now I am going to do this, I will quickly return here; I will come back to take your thought and your word. My Matron, and my Child, forgive me, have a little patience with me; I do not want to deceive you, my most abandoned Daughter, my Child. Tomorrow I will come quickly."

[75] After hearing Juan Diego's discourse, the most pious Virgin answered: "Listen and hear well in your heart, my most abandoned son: that which scares you and troubles you is nothing; do not let your countenance and heart be troubled; do not fear that sickness

or any other sickness or anxiety. [76] Am I not here, your mother? Are you not under my shadow and my protection? Am I not your source of life? Are you not in the hollow of my mantle where I cross my arms? Who else do you need?[20] [77] Let nothing trouble you or cause you sorrow. Do not worry because of your uncle's sickness. He will not die of his present sickness. Be assured in your heart that he is already healed." (And as he learned later on, at that precise moment, his uncle was healed.)

[78] When Juan Diego heard the thought and word of the Lady from Heaven, he was very much consoled; his heart became peaceful. He begged her to send him immediately to see the lord of the priests to take him his sign, the thing that would bring about the fulfillment of her desire, so that he would be believed.

[79] Then the Lady from Heaven sent him to climb to the top of the hill where he had seen her before. [80] She said to him: "Go up, my most abandoned son, to the top of the hill, and there, where you saw me and I gave you my instructions, there you will see many diverse flowers: cut them, gather them, put them together. Then come down here and bring them before me."

[81] Juan Diego climbed the hill, and when he arrived at the top, he was deeply surprised. All over the place there were all kinds of exquisite flowers from Castile, open and flowering.[21] It was not a place for flowers, and likewise it was the time when the ice hardens upon the earth. [82] They were very fragrant, as if they were filled with fine pearls, filled with the morning dew. [83] He started to cut them; he gathered them; he placed them

---

20. Notice the five identifying statements — each one deepening and expanding the meaning of the previous one. Before she had identified herself as the Mother of God; now she introduces herself as the mother of Juan Diego and of the poor; "shadow" is an image-word meaning authority; "hollow of her mantle" refers to tender service as the quality of true authority; the crossing of the arms indicates the cross of sticks that produces fire, out of which new divine life is born; Juan Diego is the firstborn of the new creation; nothing else is needed (see Siller Acuña, *Para comprender el mensaje*, 83–84).

21. Note the insistent reference to "the top of the hill" — a contrast to the top of the pyramid-temple where the old priests ascended to offer human sacrifices. Now Juan Diego (who represents the new priests) ascends to discover beautiful flowers in the place where he had first heard the heavenly music — a true place of divine-human encounter.

in the hollow of his mantle. [84] And the top of the hill was certainly not a place where flowers grew; there were only rocks, thistles, thorns, cacti, mesquites; and if small herbs grew there, during the month of December, they were all eaten up and wilted by the ice.

[85] Immediately he went down; he went to take to the Queen of Heaven the various flowers that he had cut. When she saw them, she took them in her small hands; and then he placed them in the hollow of his mantle.[22]

[86] And she told him: "My most abandoned son, these different flowers are the proof, the sign, that you will take to the bishop. In my name tell him that he is to see in them what I want, and with this he should carry out my wish and my will.

[87] "And you, you are my ambassador; in you I place all my trust.[23] With all my strength [*energía*] I command you that only in the presence of the bishop are you to open your mantle, and let him know and reveal to him what you are carrying. [88] You will recount everything well; you will tell him how I sent you to climb to the top of the hill to go cut the flowers, and all that you saw and admired. With this you will change the heart of the lord of the priests so that he will do his part to build and erect my temple that I have asked him for.

[89] As soon as the Lady from Heaven had given him her command, he immediately took to the road that leads to Mexico. He was in a hurry and very happy; his heart felt very sure and secure; he was carrying with great care what he knew would [bring about] a good end. He was very careful with that which he carried in the hollow of his mantle, less anything would fall out. He was enjoying the scent of the beautiful flowers.

---

22. He brings the flowers (truth) to her; she touches them (confirms the truth) and places them under his care. Note contrast to verse 76.

23. The Indian was considered to be unworthy of any trust, one who imagined things and easily lied and hence one who should be dominated and punished (see vv. 31, 32, 37, 38, 46, 54, 56, 57, 58, 59); the Lady from Heaven reverses this and brings out the ultimate truth about the Indians: they are the most trusted ambassadors of heaven. The Indians, who were declared unworthy of ordination by church regulations, were to be the trusted ambassadors — spokespersons — of God.

✻ Third Interview with the Bishop ✻ and the Apparition of the Virgin

[90] Upon arriving at the palace of the bishop, he ran into the doorkeepers and the other servants of the king of the priests. He begged them to go tell him [the bishop] that he wanted to see him; but none of them wanted to; they did not want to pay attention to him, both because it was still night and they knew him: he was the one who only bothered them and gave them long faces;[24] [91] and also because their fellow workers had told them how they had lost him from their sight when they had been following him. He waited for a very long time.[25]

[92] When they saw that he had been standing with his head lowered[26] (very sad) for a long time, that he was waiting in vain for them to call him, and that it seemed that he carried something in the hollow of his mantle, they approached him to see what he had and satisfy their hearts.

[93] And when Juan Diego saw that it was impossible to hide from them what he was carrying, that he would be punished for this, that they would throw him out or mistreat him, he showed them just a little of the flowers.

[94] When they saw that they were all different flowers from Castile and that it was not the season for flowers, they were very astonished, especially by the fact that they were in full bloom, so fresh, so fragrant, and very beautiful. [95] Three times they tried to grab some of them and take them from him, [96] but they could not do it because when they were about to grab them, they did not

---

24. Note the reappearance of the clause "when it was still night," which refers to the moment at which the new creation is about to begin. However, those whose livelihood and identity depend on the structures of the old creation, that is, the structures of domination, try to prevent the new creation. The rise and liberation of the poor always shake the structures of unjust domination and oppression, and those who rely on those structures try everything within their means to keep that liberation from coming about.

25. The poor and undignified of the world are always made to wait. Everyone else comes before them. It is as if they do not count.

26. In preconquest art, prisoners appeared with their heads lowered. This was indicative of their shameful condition, the condition of one who was totally subjected to the will of others.

see any more real flowers, but only painted or embroidered ones, or flowers sewn in his mantle.[27]

[97] Immediately they went to tell the lord bishop what they had seen, and that the poor little Indian who had already come many times wanted to see him, and that he had been waiting for a very long time. [98] Upon hearing this, the lord bishop realized this meant the despicable man had the proof to convince him and bring about what he was coming to ask for.

[99] Immediately he ordered that he be brought in to see him. As soon as he [Juan Diego] entered, he knelt before him [the bishop] as he had done before, and once again he told him everything he had seen and admired and also her message.

[100] He said to him: "My owner and my lord, I have accomplished what you asked for; I went to tell my Matron, my Owner, the Lady from Heaven, Holy Mary, the precious Mother of God Téotl, how you had asked me for a sign in order to believe me, so that you might build her temple where she is asking you to erect it. [101] And besides, I told her that I had given you my word that I would bring you a sign and a proof of her will that you want to receive from my hands. When she received your thought and your word, she accepted willingly what you asked for, a sign and a proof so that her desire and will may come about.

[102] "And today when it was still night, she sent me to come and see you once again. But I asked her for the sign and the proof of her will that you asked me for and that she had agreed to give to me. Immediately she complied.

[103] "She sent me to the top of the hill, where I had seen her before, so that there I might cut the flowers from Castile. After I had cut them, I took them to the bottom of the hill. And she, with her precious little hands, took them; she arranged them in the hollow of my mantle, so that I might bring them to you, and deliver them to you personally. [104] Even though I knew well that the top of the hill was not a place where flowers grow, that only

---

27. In Nahuatl, "sewn in his mantle" meant something had become part of one's innermost being.

stones, thistles, thorns, cacti and mesquites abound there, I still was neither surprised nor doubted. [105] As I was arriving at the top of the hill, my eyes became fixed: It was the Flowering Earth![28] It was covered with all kinds of flowers from Castile, full of dew and shinning brilliantly. Immediately I went to cut them. [106] And she told me why I had to deliver them to you: so that you might see the sign you requested and so that you will believe in her will; and also so that the truth of my word and my message might be manifested. Here they are. Please receive them."

[107] He unfolded his white mantle, the mantle in whose hollow he had gathered the flowers he had cut, and at that instant the different flowers from Castile fell to the ground. In that very moment she painted herself: the precious image of the Ever-Virgin Holy Mary, Mother of the God Téotl, appeared suddenly, just as she is today and is kept in her precious home, in her hermitage of Tepeyac, which is called Guadalupe.[29]

✳ Conversion of the Bishop ✳

[108] When the lord bishop saw her, he and all who accompanied him fell to their knees and were greatly astonished. They stood up to see her; they became saddened; their hearts and their minds became very heavy.

[109] The lord bishop, with tears and sadness, prayed to her and begged her to forgive him for not having believed her will, her heart, and her word.

[110] When he stood up, he untied the mantle from Juan Diego's neck, the mantle in which had appeared and was painted the Lady from Heaven. Then he took her and went to place her in his oratory.

---

28. "Flowering Earth" was the Nahuatl expression for the place where ultimate truth resides.
29. See footnote 1, p. 5 above.

✳ The Construction of the Hermitage ✳

[111] Juan Diego spent one more day in the home of the bishop, who had invited him [to stay]. And on the next day he said: "Let us go to see where it is the will of the Lady from Heaven that the hermitage be built."

[112] Immediately people were invited to construct and build it. And when Juan Diego showed where the Lady from Heaven had indicated that the hermitage should be built, he asked permission to leave. [113] He wanted to go home to see his uncle Juan Bernardino, the one who had been in his final agony, whom he had left to go to Tlatelolco to call a priest to come, hear his confession, and prepare him well, the one who, the Lady from Heaven had said, had been healed. But they did not let him go alone; they accompanied him to his home.

✳ The Fourth Apparition and First Miracle ✳

[114] When they arrived, they saw his uncle who was well and with no pains. [115] He [Juan Bernardino] was very much surprised that his nephew was so well accompanied and honored, and he asked him why they were honoring him so much.

[116] He told him how when he had left him to go call a priest to come to hear his confession and prepare him well, the Queen of Heaven appeared to him over there, at Tepeyac, and sent him to Mexico to see the lord bishop so that he would build her a home at Tepeyac. [117] And she told him not to be troubled because his uncle was healed, and he was very consoled.

[118] And the uncle said that this was true, that it was precisely then that she had healed him, and he had seen her exactly as she had shown herself to his nephew, and that she had told him that he [Juan Bernardino] had to go to Mexico to see the bishop. [119] And [she told him] also that when he went to see the bishop, he would reveal all that he had seen and would tell him in what a marvelous way she had healed him and that he [the bishop] would

call and name that precious image the Ever-Virgin Holy Mary of Guadalupe.

[120] They took Juan Bernardino to the bishop so that he might speak and witness before him. [121] And, together with his nephew Juan Diego, he was hosted by the bishop in his home for several days, until the hermitage of the Queen and Lady from Heaven was built at Tepeyac, where Juan Diego had seen her.

✳ The Entire City before the Virgin ✳

[122] And the lord bishop transferred to the major church the precious image of the Queen and Lady from Heaven; he took her from the oratory of his palace so that all might see and venerate her precious image.

[123] The entire city was deeply moved; they came to see and admire her precious image as something divine; they came to pray to her. [124] They admired very much how she had appeared as a divine marvel, because absolutely no one on earth had painted her precious image.

Part 11

THE GUADALUPAN
ENCOUNTER

* * *

– 1 –

When It Was Still Night

It was Saturday, when it was still night . . . (v. 7)

The Time and Space

For the ancient Nahuatls, time was of the very essence of persons, of events, and of the cosmic process that brought about the ends and beginnings of civilizations. The author of the Guadalupe story is very careful to situate us in the precise moment of this extraordinary happening. It is very much like St. Luke wanting to situate the birth of the Savior of the world at the very precise moment of the census ordered by Caesar Augustus.

It was a moment of death and darkness, a moment of desolation and tears, a moment of chaos and confusion:

Ten years after the conquest of the city of Mexico, arrows and shields were put down; everywhere the inhabitants of the lake and the mountain had surrendered. (v. 3)

Having carefully stated the fact of the conquest, whose details, like those of the crucifixion, were too bloody, painful, and shameful to want to describe, the author of our poem goes on to note carefully that *"it was Saturday, when it was still night"* (v. 7). The precise time is crucial for understanding the historical and cosmic implications that this event had for those who first experienced it.

The time is 1531. The place is the city of Mexico — site of what had been the most developed, advanced, and well-organized civilization of pre-Columbian America, a city now reduced to ashes,

25

its canals filled with corpses, its streets filled with people moving around as if they were the living dead. It was the epicenter of the great cultural earthquake that had destroyed the entire edifice of native civilizations. The previously highly disciplined people were now wandering around aimlessly, with no life, purpose, or direction. The warriors had been killed or reduced to humiliating servitude; their women had been violated; their beautiful cities had been burned; and their gods were being destroyed.[1] Their old ways were being discredited, and the new ways did not make sense to them. Nothing of meaning or value was left; there was no reason to live. And on top of all this, the Europeans had brought new diseases that devastated the remaining population, making the stench of death the constant companion of everyday existence.

It is difficult, maybe even impossible, for us today to comprehend the magnitude of the desolation. This was the most painful and chaotic period of the postconquest years, a period that had started with the colossal defeat of the Aztec peoples, which had then led to the defeat of the entire native population and their way of life. It was a time of collective trauma among the entire native population — the horrors of their destruction were all around, and those who had not died were in a state of shock. The conquest of Mexico had started on Good Friday 1519, and now that long and arduous way of the cross of the native Mexicans had come to its crucifixion.[2] Their gods had been absent when they needed them most; their gods had turned silent and died! They would now be a people without life — without a life of their own.

Conquest, bloodshed, and destruction were nothing new to the warrior culture of the Aztecs or, for that matter, to the history of humanity at large. In this regard, it might be helpful to compare the Aztecs to the Israelites at the time of King Solomon. First, each had been a nomadic people, had undergone a pilgrimage

---

1. For an excellent discussion of the impact of the conquest on women, see María Pilar Aquino, *Our Cry for Life: A Feminist Theology from Latin America* (Maryknoll, N.Y.: Orbis Books, 1993), 13–18.

2. For a devotional meditation on the cross of the peoples of the Americas, see Virgil Elizondo, *Way of the Cross: Passion of Christ in the Americas* (Maryknoll, N.Y.: Orbis Books, 1992).

(the Aztecs had wandered from Aztlán) to the Valley of Mexico, had conquered peoples who occupied the promised land they wanted, and had established glorious temple-cities (Jerusalem and Tenochtitlán). Second, like the Israelites, the Aztecs had let their pride and grandeur get the best of them, had forgotten their own struggles, and had oppressed even their own people. To the degree that they prospered and conquered, the hatred and resentment of their enemies increased, and the daily burdens they imposed upon the masses of simple working people of their societies increased. As we know from any great civilization, and the Aztecs and Israelites of Solomon's time were among the greatest, grandeur exacts a terrible price and cannot exist without the oppression and exploitation of the masses. Third, the Aztecs were similar to the chosen people of Hebrew Scripture in their conviction that they were God's chosen people.

However, here the comparison ends. The Hebrews, after all, did not practice human sacrifice. Further, unlike the Israelites, the Aztecs' evolution and development came to an abrupt end with the destruction of their temple-city, Tenochtitlán, and the attempted destruction of their religion. Finally, after the apparent destruction of the Aztecs' gods, no prophets emerged from among them to purify and develop their own religion,[3] and no messiah appeared to save them from their enemies and oppressors. It appeared that they were left totally alone and destined to die as aliens in their own lands, in the lands of their parents and ancestors.

The Aztecs had built a massive empire and one of the most beautiful cities the world had ever known. They were proud of their achievements as the people chosen by their gods to perpetuate the existence of the sun, the source of life. War, self-discipline, hard work, sacrifice, technology, imagination, and religion had led them to be a powerful and glorious people. These elements were

---

3. In effect, the theological-political dimension of the Aztec religion was just beginning to develop and be elaborated among the *tlamatini* (wise men/theologians) of that period. They were moving away from human sacrifice and were searching for new possibilities in the mystery of the "One through whom We Live" — a term also used by Our Lady in presenting herself to Juan Diego, thus distancing herself from the gods of human sacrifice. See Richard Nebel, *Santa María Tonantzin: Virgen de Guadalupe* (Mexico City: Fondo de Cultura Económica, 1995), 84.

intimately interconnected with one another. Human struggle lived
out in war and symbolized by their war gods had become the very
essence of their life, and their able young men were educated from
boyhood in the art and science of warfare for the sake of cosmic
harmony.

The Aztecs had become a great civilization not just because of
their bravery and military might but also because of their syn-
cretistic nature.[4] They were not afraid to learn from and to make
their own the cultural heritage of the very peoples they conquered.
In that process, however, they assimilated these heritages through
the militaristic-theocentric cultural grid that was the very essence
of their identity and mission. The gods had sacrificed themselves
to bring about human life, so it was humans' obligation to offer human sacrifice to maintain the cosmic harmony of creation.
For many of the other nations and religions of ancient Mexico,
the Aztec cosmovision that demanded human sacrifice was a perversion of the will of the god Quetzalcoatl, who had demanded
self-abnegation and penance but prohibited human sacrifice.

The Aztecs did not destroy all traces of the gods of their captives
but rather took them into their own pantheon and even erected a
temple to all the gods—like the Greeks' Areopagus. Their guiding
principle of progress and development was that they were enriched
by what they learned and received from the others, including their
gods. They absorbed others' technological know-how, their philosophy, their wisdom, their arts and crafts, and everything else
that would better and enrich Aztec civilization. As they grew and
developed and their cities and empires became more complex, so
did their hierarchical socioreligious structures—in a process similar to the growth of our own religious institutional structures.
Soon, a very rigid hierarchy of social roles developed that, inter-
preted through their theocentric culture, made everyone slaves of
the gods.

The conquest of 1521 was radically different from and infinitely
more devastating than any conquest by the Aztecs or other peoples
in pre-Columbian America. The European conquerors were not in-

---

4. Nebel, *Santa María Tonantzin*, 81.

corporating the Aztec gods. Quite the opposite, their gods, their religion, and the ways of their ancestors were being discredited, insulted, maligned, and totally destroyed. All their connections to the sources of life were being smashed. They could accept being conquered and dominated by a new power, but they could not accept the absolute break with the ways of their ancestors and the destruction of their gods. Like other conquerors, the Christians burned the conquered people's temples and imposed their gods. But they refused any sharing, demanded the annihilation of local cults, and kept for themselves an absolute monopoly of the priesthood and the sacred.[5] This radical opposition to everything that had been sacred to Indian people was the deepest source of their collective trauma. Montezuma accepted the sovereignty of the Spanish king, but he would not under any circumstances renounce his religion and neither would Cuauhtemoc, the noblest epic figure in the history of the Americas, a figure who continues to be one of the most popular folk heroes of Mexican culture.[6]

At this moment of history, the people not only had been defeated militarily but had been vanquished spiritually. They had given up — they appeared to have no choice; there appeared to be no other way; and any attempt even to suggest change or opposition was immediately suppressed with the greatest brutality.[7] The great church historian Justo González comments on this moment of human history:

> I am convinced that the so-called "encounter" between two hemispheres led to one of the greatest tragedies in human history, and one of the worst blots on Christian history. The death of millions upon millions of human beings, the disappearance of entire civilizations and peoples, and the subjugation of others for five hundred years should not be

5. Serge Gruzinski, *The Conquest of Mexico* (New York: Polity Press, 1993), 151.

6. See Justo Sierra, *The Political Evolution of the Mexican People* (Austin: University of Texas Press, 1969), 58–60.

7. Miguel León-Portilla, *Endangered Cultures* (Dallas: Southern Methodist University Press, 1990), 71–97; and Serge Gruzinski, *La guerre des images* (Paris: Fayard, 1990), 29.

obscured nor minimized. The cries of trampled and destroyed generations still rise to heaven, and justice still remains to be done.[8]

I have no doubt that for the Indian world this period of history appeared as the absolute apocalyptic end of not only their collective life but their entire history. They and their entire past were being wiped out.

The Historical Night

There are important elements in the poem that prepare us for the very special Nahuatl meaning of *"night."* The first is that in verse 3 we are told that the inhabitants had surrendered — that is, there were no more wars. They had put down their *"arrows and shields."*[9] That sounds simple enough to us, but it was not so simple for the Nahuatl world. For the native peoples, life consisted of the harmonious union of various contradictory tensions. Hence, life meant constant struggles. This was expressed through the various "wars" they engaged in — whether "wars of flowers" (simulated battles) or wars for captives. War was not necessarily a military campaign. It signified the struggle for life of the individual, the group, and all the elements of creation. Thus *"they had surrendered"* meant there was no more struggle, no more energy, no more life. Life had come to an end.[10]

This was the time of the dark night of the collective soul of the Indian nations. Their warriors had been killed, their temples destroyed, their women raped, their people forced into harsh work, and now they were told their gods were not true. The people had

---

8. Justo González, "Voices of Compassion," *Missiology* 20, no. 2 (1992): 163.

9. Some translations have the word "peace" instead of "surrender." If there was peace, it was not a dynamic and life-giving peace. Rather, it was a peace characterized by having no choice and having to accept an absolute, shameful, and total surrender — giving up everything that had been of value, including the native people's religion. It was the peace not of a free people but of an oppressed and dominated people who had no choice but to submit or be punished or killed.

10. Clodomiro L. Siller Acuña, "El método de evangelización en el Nican Mopohua," *Servir* 17, nos. 93–94 (1981): 268.

gone from being the lords and ladies of their destiny to being humiliated, crushed, and now destined to be the nameless and faceless servants of the foreigners. They were engulfed in a darkness constituted by pain; by the dying cries of a people who were not only physically defeated but also psychologically crushed and spiritually vanquished; by humiliation and the subsequent shame of being a people whose gods had been defeated; by shame for the ancestral sin that had merited such a painful humiliation and severe punishment. It was the dark world of people bent over with hard work and insulting treatment. It was the darkness of nothingness. It was a living nightmare, and death seemed the only escape. Everything good and meaningful had been destroyed and replaced by a cruel and totally incomprehensible reality:

> Many Indians hang themselves, others let themselves die of hunger, others poison themselves with herbs, there are mothers who kill their children to whom they have just given birth, saying that they are doing it to spare them the trials that they are enduring.[11]

The once-proud Aztec warriors and builders of one of the greatest city-civilizations the world had ever known were now reduced to something less than human. Those who had known themselves to be the people chosen by the gods to ensure the survival of the cosmic order were now reduced to scared and miserable beings. The painful psalms of the immediate postconquest period bring this out:

> The lamentations increase, tears flow everywhere.
> Cry, my friends,
> and understand that with these events
> we have lost the Mexican nation.
> The waters have turned into acid, the food has become acidified.
> This is what the giver of life in Tlatelolco has done.[12]

---

11. Taken from *Cédula Real* of May 1582, as quoted by Gruzinski, *The Conquest of Mexico*, 97.

12. Quoted in Miguel León-Portilla, *Visión de los vencidos* (Mexico City: UNAM, 1972), 165.

The once-great and thriving Mexican nation was finished. What else could the native Mexicans do but cry and disappear into nothingness? They had built one of the greatest and most beautiful cities — with flourishing marketplaces, flower gardens, and imposing buildings — yet now it was reduced to ashes, blood-stained walls, worm-eaten corpses, rancid waters, and putrid food, if there was any food at all. There was no answer for their ultimate question: What has the God of life done? They cried out:

> Allow us to die, allow us to perish,
> since our gods have already died.[13]

The Cosmic Night

In our poem, the historical time of what appeared as an eternal darkness of suffering, confusion, disorientation, and total chaos is now linked to the cosmic rhythm of ongoing creations. This is not just a moment of history; this is not just another military or religious conquest; this is not just another invasion in the history of the many invasions of the world. We are now in a moment of cosmic time! The Nahuatl cosmovision was structured around successive creations — each one preceded by massive disasters. We are now in a key moment in the cosmic movement of the universe, when a massive cataclysm will be followed by a new creation. We are now in one of those rare moments of human experience when the cosmic will triumph over the historic, and we will be there to participate in this triumph.

The phrase *"when it was still night"* (when dawn had not yet started) is a classical Nahuatl expression for the moment in mythical time immediately before creation. It was the time when the gods were deliberating about the new humanity that they were to bring about. According to the Indians' ancient beliefs, the world had gone through severe cataclysms that disrupted and destroyed everything that was — civilizations, valleys, and mountains. But

---

13. From the *Coloquios y doctrina cristiana*, as recorded by Bernardino de Sahagún, quoted from León-Portilla, *Endangered Cultures*.

after each such gigantic cataclysm, the gods, *"when it was still night,"* had deliberated and decided to begin anew. The Aztecs had been living during the period of the fifth creation, called by them the Fifth Sun. From their reading of the signs of earth and sky, they were convinced their time was coming to an end. In fact, many scholars today are convinced this was one of the decisive forces that kept the native inhabitants from fighting more fiercely against the Spaniards from the very beginning. They were defeated even before the battles started.

Now the cyclic creations that the Aztecs believed in would once again be experienced by the people at large. What had appeared as the tragic end would now appear as the moment of creation: as the night-struggle out of which a new creation would erupt. As stated above, in the Nahuatl cosmovision, *"when it was still night"* is an image used for the origins of creation. The image appears several times in the narrative. The author wants to emphasize the uniqueness of the moment. It is the moment of origins — like the "darkness" or "formless wasteland" of Gen. 1:1 or the nighttime of Luke 2:8 when Jesus was born. Thus we are here at an event as important as the creation of the world and as significant as the birth of the one who redeemed it. In the Nahuatl reading of cyclic creations, we might well call this the beginning of the Sixth Sun. This is the moment when the dramatic birth of a new humanity is about to take place; it is a cosmic moment of creation.

Juan Diego, a low-class mission Indian, appears out of the darkness of the night. It is not just the physical darkness before dawn. It was the darkness of one who has been made ashamed of one's very being, who is bent over with the weight of hard work and humiliating treatment. It is the lifeless darkness of the smoke emanating from the ashes of a defeated and burned city. But when Juan Diego arrives at Tepeyac, there is a radical new beginning — from the darkness of nothingness to the darkness of expectation. Juan Diego leaves his home *"when it was still night"* but arrives at Tepeyac while *"it was already beginning to dawn"* (v. 8). Tepeyac will be the site of the new creation. It is here that a new humanity will begin. This will not be a new conquest but a new creation.

– 2 –

It Was Already Beginning to Dawn

And when he arrived at the side of the small hill, which was named Tepeyac, it was already beginning to dawn. (v. 8)

"*Beginning to dawn*" is the other side of "*when it was still night.*" Thus we are here witnessing the beginning of the new creation. All the imagery and movement of the narrative bring out the divine initiative that invites and collaborates with the defeated Indian to initiate something truly new — new for the Indian world, new for the Spanish world, new for humanity. The missioners had been working and praying for the success of their evangelizing mission. Now their prayers would be answered, but not in the way they had planned or in ways they had suspected.

The Singing of the Birds: Cosmic Awakening

He heard singing on the summit of the hill: as if different precious birds were singing and their songs would alternate, as if the hill was answering them. Their song was most pleasing and very enjoyable, better than that of the coyoltotol or of the tzinizcan or of the other precious birds that sing. (v. 9)

If people in the Nahuatl world wanted to speak about divine revelation, they would refer to it in terms of "flower and song," for mere human discourse was never sufficient to communicate about the divine. The Nahuatl theologians stated: "It may be that no one

34

on earth can tell the truth, except through flower and song."[1] Rational discourse clarifies yet limits the mind, while flowers and song stimulate the imagination to ponder the infinite. For the Nahuatl, it was only through poetic communication and beauty that the heart of human beings could enter into communion and communication with the divine — both individually and collectively. For the Nahuatl, truth was expressed through the suggestive harmony of the seen and heard. Through the beauty of the image (flowers) and the melodious sounds (poetic word), the divine could be gradually experienced, and one could gradually come to share in the divine wisdom. Thus the Guadalupe event marks the opening of a divine-human encounter and of a divine communication. This harmony, this symmetry, was an essential element of the Nahuatl vision and hence of this revelatory poem. All must be in balance — words, images, numbers. For instance, the number of times a word is used in a phrase is part of the meaning of the phrase — the meaning resides not just in the words but also in how many times they are used and how they are arranged.

The adventure begins with the beautiful and alluring singing of the birds. Juan Diego freely and happily goes to the source of the singing. It is so beautiful that he cannot resist going to its source. Nobody threatens him or demands that he go. It is so attractive that he freely and joyfully goes. The fact that there are five references to song in this time and space indicates — in the Nahuatl mode of communication — that we are at the very center of creation, where heaven meets earth. The number five emphasizes the beauty of the song, indicating the beginning of a perfectly composed divine communication. Thus Juan Diego is drawn toward the realm of the divine. He had been on his way to Tlatelolco to learn about God, but here he hears God speaking in the language of his people: in beautiful singing. The way he expresses this experience lets us know that he certainly knew he was in the realm of a divine communication.[2]

---

1. From "Cantares mexicanos," folio 13, as quoted in Miguel León-Portilla, *Aztec Thought and Culture* (Norman: University of Oklahoma Press, 1963), 83.

2. Clodomiro L. Siller Acuña, *Para comprender el mensaje de María de Guadalupe* (Buenos Aires: Editorial Guadalupe, 1989), 62.

Juan Diego is no naive dummy; he is no fool who will be easily taken in by the mere workings of his imagination or the beautiful feeling that the music has brought about. He is no mere passive recipient. He is perplexed by the situation and wonders what it is all about. In the midst of this incredibly beautiful experience, so beautiful that he thinks he is in heaven, he pauses to ask the crucial questions:

> *"By chance do I deserve this? Am I worthy of what I am hearing? Maybe I am dreaming? Maybe I only see this in my dreams? Where am I?"* (v. 10)

Juan Diego raises five possible objections. This, according to the Nahuatl mode of communication, indicates that he is assured that he is not imagining things and that what he is experiencing is really happening. Having assured himself of the authenticity of his experience, he now radicalizes his quest. After all, the missioners, "God's messengers," were demanding that the Indians break with the ways of their ancestors, that they abandon their ancient customs and traditions, that they totally erase from their minds all their religious ideas. Now, in the midst of this experience of the divine, he dares to ask:

> *"Maybe I am in the land of my ancestors, of the elders, of our grandparents? In the Land of Flower, in the Earth of our flesh? Maybe over there inside of heaven?"* (v. 11)

Now he knows that he is in contact and in continuity with the very tradition (i.e., the "ancestors") that had given birth to his people, that he is in contact with real and unquestioned truth (i.e., the "flower"), and that he is in a place that surpasses every other place on earth (i.e., "heaven") in beauty, truth, and goodness. But weren't the missioners opposed to all this? Would the priests punish him if they found out about this experience?[3] Even though the

---

3. Punishment, even with death, of Indians who proposed such ideas was not uncommon and later on would be proposed for the one who introduced the idea of Our Lady of Guadalupe. Several Indian leaders had been put to death for proposing similar ideas. See Miguel León-Portilla, *Endangered Cultures* (Dallas: Southern Methodist University Press, 1990), 72–81; and Richard Nebel, *Santa María To-*

poem does not explicitly state that Juan Diego was puzzled, we can detect it in the questions he asks. His puzzlement is like that of Mary upon the greeting of the angel Gabriel: "She was deeply troubled by his words and wondered what his greeting meant" (Luke 1:29). Something truly divine is beginning, but at this point Juan Diego does not know where it will lead or even what will happen to him.

At this point of the Nahuatl poem, there are not yet any flowers (the other element of the divine communication); thus we know that the communication is just beginning. Juan Diego will have to collaborate to complete the divine communication. This is truly something new: it is a cosmic event, but it will be completed through the cooperation of a historical human being. Juan Diego is drawn to the divinely chosen center of creation to be invited to collaborate in this new divine-human endeavor. It is the annunciation of what is about to begin. The beautiful singing of the birds is equivalent to the angel Gabriel's calling, "Rejoice, highly favored," to Mary (Luke 1:28). Like Mary of Nazareth, Juan Diego is invited to cooperate in God's project for humanity. He finds himself in the presence of the divine. It is so beautiful that he feels he is in heaven, in the land of his ancestors, in the place of ultimate truth, in the very womb of human life.[4] Here, he is in the brilliant and glorious presence of ultimate truth — which is equally the place of ultimate beauty, not the artificial beauty of the Aztec temples or of the cathedrals and palaces of New Spain, but the beauty of the land out of which the people were born and carved their daily existence.

This contrast is between the inviting beauty of the heavenly call and the chilling and paralyzing fear provoked by the human sacrifices of the Aztecs or by the threats of hell and damnation of the missioners. The missioners punished Indians who did not come to religious instructions or who fell asleep during the long explanations of Christianity. They beat them with rods, imprisoned them, and put them in chains to teach them the Christian doctrine.[5]

---

nantzin: Virgen de Guadalupe (Mexico City: Fondo de Cultura Económica, 1995), 127.

4. Siller Acuña, *Para comprender el mensaje,* 62–63.

5. See Robert Ricard, *The Spiritual Conquest of Mexico: The Evangelizing*

The missioners tried to physically beat the Indians into believing in God's love and mercy while the Indians' own native religions sought captives to sacrifice to the gods. At Tepeyac, there is no need for this horrible nonsense. The beautiful singing is a joyful invitation that Juan Diego quickly and fully responds to without the need of any threats — very much like the response of the apostles to the call of Jesus in the Gospels, like the response today of the people who come to church not because of threats or demands of church regulations but because of the beautiful singing, the exciting rituals, and the inviting words of the Gospels.[6]

Mount Tepeyac: The Womb

The encounter takes place on Mount Tepeyac,[7] which was far away from the Aztec capital where human sacrifices had taken place and where the natives had been defeated and massacred. It was far away from the great imperial capital of the Aztecs that was now becoming New Spain's center of power and oppression. One empire was replacing another, but for the poor of the land, nothing ever changes, for regardless who is on top, they continue to be crushed, shamed, abused, and exploited — even to this day.

The missioners and their centers of evangelization and learning played a very ambiguous role in the lives and future of the natives. The intention and efforts of the missioners were to help the Indians enter into the universal orbit of humanity through conversion to Christianity. This was a great and very noble goal, but the way they sought to achieve it was disastrous. They worked hard to create spaces where the Indians could feel at home among their own, but always under the supervision and tutelage of the missioners. The early missioners made heroic efforts to understand and pro-

---

Methods of the Mendicant Orders in New Spain, 1523–1572, trans. Lesley Byrd Simpson (Berkeley: University of California Press, 1966), 96.

6. This will be the subject matter of my next book, now in the final stages of preparation.

7. For a good presentation of the various significations of Tepeyac for the ancient cultures of the Americas, see Ed Sylvest, *Nuestra Señora de Guadalupe, Mother of God* (Dallas: Southern Methodist University Press, 1992), 1–8.

mote much of the Indian way of life.[8] People like Pedro de Gante organized the first schools for Indians, produced the first catechism in Nahuatl, and started the tradition of Indian-European art; Vasco de Quiroga constructed evangelical towns; Bartolomé de las Casas saw the providence of God (rather than demons) in the ways of the natives. A few of the missioners, especially the earlier ones, loved and admired many of the Indians' values, customs, languages, and practices and wanted not only to understand those things better but to help the Indians maintain them, though they were to be maintained only in forms that harmonized with Christian religion.

The schools were set up for the children both of the nobility and of the ordinary people so that they could learn Latin, philosophy, grammar, and other subjects. The Indian children learned faster than the Spanish, and thus the schools were soon closed — the Indians' demonstration of their intelligence was too much of a threat to Spanish power and domination. Further, though some missioners promoted the education of the Indians, a good number of the missioners were opposed and hostile to the education of the natives because they considered them incapable and unworthy of learning.[9]

The children chosen to attend these schools were taken away from their families, from their cultural way of life, and from their ordinary surroundings and were forced to live like monks.[10] They had to abandon their people in every way to become good and successful students. Regardless of the good intentions of the missioners, the Indians never felt at home in these institutions, and their difference was constantly reinforced in many subtle and open ways. I can well understand this, for this has been the experience of many of our Mexican-Americans and Latinos in the schools and especially seminaries and convents of the United States, and this sense of alienation has been even more profound for Native

---

8. Besides the persons mentioned below, these included humanists like Andrés de Olmos, Bernardino de Sahagún, Gerónimo de Mediata, and others among the first waves of missioners. See León-Portilla, *Endangered Cultures*, 85–96, 103–6.

9. Ricard, *The Spiritual Conquest of Mexico*, 225ff.

10. Ricard, *The Spiritual Conquest of Mexico*, 218ff.

Americans who have been brought into "American" schools and institutions.

A few of the children of the former Aztec princes and noble families were invited to the Colegio de la Santa Cruz for formal education, but even there the contrasts between the conquering Spaniards and the defeated Indians deepened and solidified. Great missioners such as Sahagún investigated the way of life of the natives with great diligence, but their ultimate purpose was to show them where they were wrong.[11] The European education of the natives reinforced their inferiority not because they could not learn — for, in effect, they were learning faster and better than the Spaniards — but because the Europeans taught about European ways as if they were the only ways of becoming a true human being. Education meant discrediting the ways of the natives as pagan and uncivilized in favor of the Christian and "civilized" ways of the newly installed dominant group. Here the natives came to serve, obey, and learn from those who claimed they had the monopoly on all truth — cultural and religious. When the natives became Christians, they became foreigners to their own people while never being fully accepted into the inner circle of the conquering Europeans.

In the new capital, the new cultural hegemony was quickly solidifying: the Europeans as models of the new humanity, the university to teach their ways, and their religious to give divine legitimacy to the entire enterprise.[12] At Tlatelolco, the new center of religious power and learning, the natives were not at home; in fact, it was the place where "native home" was driven out of them in the name of God and civilization.[13] They were in a strange

---

11. Ricard, *The Spiritual Conquest of Mexico,* 40.

12. Ricard, *The Spiritual Conquest of Mexico,* 217–35.

13. I experienced this recently in a workshop I conducted on inculturation for leaders of some of the North American Indian nations. Many recounted personal experiences of how missioners (Catholic and Protestant) had taken them away from their families to "Christian-Indian schools" where everything about their families and ancestors was discredited as pagan, inferior, and uncivilized. "Home" was driven out of them, and since they were never fully accepted into the Euro-American societies, they will, thanks to the missioners, always remain homeless people, no matter how good the housing facilities might be. All these leaders felt the missioners had separated and alienated them from their families — and yet today we make

and alien place that was designed to remake their bodies and souls into something they were not — Euro-Christians. The more educated they became, the more ashamed they became of the ways of their ancestors and the more alienated they became from their own people, knowing all the while, however, that they would never be fully accepted as true equals in the ranks of the white Europeans. It was education unto inferiority. This happened in all the Christian-Indian schools (Protestant or Catholic) throughout the Americas.[14] For European missioners, and many of today's North American missioners, cultural conversion has been seen either as a prerequisite to conversion to Christianity or at least as necessary for the proper growth, development, and maturation of the faith.[15]

If, on the cultural level, the Spanish and the Mexicans had mutually scandalized each other based on their individual approaches to violence and killing human beings, then on the religious level, real dialogue and unity would be rendered impossible by the Spaniards' obsession with doctrinal (conceptual) purity and the Mexicans' inability to separate the religion of their ancestors from their culture. Given the religious climate of sixteenth-century Spain, the missioners felt and expressed a violent aversion to everything and anything that appeared to be linked to the indigenous religions.[16] For the Spaniards, all things associated with the Indian religions were repugnant, abominable, and could be traced to the work of the devil. Europeans of that period were obsessed with demons and saw them everywhere. Thus no matter how much some missioners tried to respect the Indian culture (and many did not) together with all its fascinating artistic, linguistic, and philosophical values, by attempting to destroy its religious base, they were in effect destroying the root, cohesiveness, and common destiny of the native peoples. Hence even in the best and most welcoming of Spanish institutions,

---

family life the cornerstone of our mission and preaching.... The very tight family life we destroyed we are now trying to promote.

14. George Tinker, *Missionary Conquest: The Gospel and Native American Cultural Genocide* (Minneapolis: Fortress Press, 1993).

15. Tinker, *Missionary Conquest,* 46ff.

16. León-Portilla, *Endangered Cultures,* 98ff.; Casiano Floristán, "Evangelization of the 'New World': An Old World Perspective," *Missiology* 20, no. 2 (1992): 137–38.

Indians did not feel at home. As María Pilar Aquino points out: "The Europeans never asked the indigenous people how they had organized themselves for centuries or how they wished to organize themselves in this new situation. They simply imposed their own models."[17]

In becoming a Christian according to the Spanish model and Spanish ecclesial demands of that period, Juan Diego was abandoning his people culturally. He was on the way to becoming a foreigner among his own people — never to be fully accepted by European society while at the same time being distanced and even alienated from his own people.

Tepeyac was still a place where the natives could be alone (away from the foreign masters) and at home in familiar surroundings. At Tepeyac, Juan Diego appears to be comfortable and secure. He appears to have no doubts about who he is and does not seem to be intimidated in the presence of the Lady of Tepeyac (in contrast to his intimidation in the presence of the bishop in the episcopal palace). In Tepeyac, he is at home while in Mexico/Tlatelolco he is ill at ease, fearful, and an alien in his own land. In verse 11 he proclaims what he experiences at Tepeyac: he feels like he is in the land of his ancestors, his grandparents; in the "Land of Flower" (i.e., the land of truth); in the "Earth of our flesh" (i.e., in the presence of the Lord of life who forms us in the wombs of our mothers). He is in heaven, in a place of transcendence. Here is the place where ultimate truth will be made manifest.[18] But most of all, here he is truly at home; here he can be himself; here he does not have to be ashamed of who he is, of how he dresses, of how he speaks or looks, of the beloved and revered ways of his ancestors.

All persons from a "minority" who have had to explain themselves and even their existence — often in a foreign tongue — to the dominant group can certainly understand immediately the deep feeling of freedom and belonging that Juan Diego experiences at Tepeyac. In a foreign land, just a favorite song in one's own language immediately brings forth deep sensations of connectedness

---

17. María Pilar Aquino, *Our Cry for Life: A Feminist Theology from Latin America* (Maryknoll, N.Y.: Orbis Books, 1993), 47.

18. Siller Acuña, *Para comprender el mensaje,* 63.

and belonging. Tepeyac had not been taken away from the Indian people. Here Juan Diego is not bombarded with foreign words and strange demands—he is truly at home in the land that had always belonged to his people.

Tepeyac had been left alone because the conquerors saw it as having no economic importance. Yet for the native peoples, it was one of the most sacred sites of the Americas. It was the sacred mountain of Tonantzin, where the feminine aspect of the deity had been venerated for many generations. It had been a pilgrimage site from time immemorial.[19] For the native world, God could not be God if there was not both a masculine and a feminine aspect. Otherwise God would not be complete.[20] The missioners were promoting the Father of Heaven; the natives would provide the Mother of Earth. Now God's creation could be complete: heaven and earth; mother and father.

Mount Tepeyac is a place of both continuity and transformation. It is the place where the Mother God regenerates life: out of the old that has passed away, new life will emerge. It is the place where earth touches heaven, or better yet, where the human is touched by the divine. In this encounter, the ultimate truth about God and human beings becomes evident, and through this revealed truth, everyone will be transformed.

In the Aztec and other Meso-American civilizations, the native priests and their victims ascended to the top of the pyramid-temples to perform the human sacrifices that were to guarantee the perpetuation of life. Juan Diego ascends to the top of the mountain-temple not to be sacrificed or to sacrifice anyone else, but to discover himself as God sees him: as a mature, dignified, and trusted person.[21] At Tepeyac, there are no victims; there is only the comforting beauty of the divine presence. Here no one will sacrifice anyone else: neither on an altar nor on a battlefield

---

19. Sylvest, *Nuestra Señora de Guadalupe*, 1–8.

20. León-Portilla, *Aztec Thought and Culture;* and Clodomiro L. Siller Acuña, "Para una teología del Nican Mopohua," *Servir* 12, no. 62 (1976): 161.

21. Even though, after much debate in Spain, the natives had been accepted as "human beings," they were considered and defined to be "minors" — people who had not arrived at the age of reason. See Floristán, "Evangelization of the 'New World': An Old World Perspective," 143.

nor through harsh labor. Yet there is total transformation. The one crushed, humiliated, and silenced by Europe is transformed into the respected, valued, and dignified Juan Diego. Juan Diego feels secure, without fear, and very happy (v. 14). All the mesquites, cacti, and even stones around Tepeyac radiate beauty like the most precious feathers and stones he had ever seen (v. 18). The contrast here is most striking: between the death stench and chaos of the valley of the imperial city of Mexico and the celestial glory of the deserted Tepeyac.

He was going to Tlatelolco to learn about God from the newly arrived European priests, who told him they were the image of God the Father.[22] To become a priest of the new religion of Tlatelolco, one had to be ordained. The Spanish missionaries never called natives to their priesthood — they would never be considered good enough. They would not be allowed to wear the vestments of the men who claimed to be "the image of God the Father." They would never be allowed into the inner sanctum of the new religion. Baptized, yes, but ordained or professed, no. The ultimate reason for this rejection was that "they preserved many values and customs of their native mothers."[23]

The seeds of the gospel were indeed planted, but their germination and full growth were prevented by this Eurocentric prohibition. As I mentioned earlier, this prohibition continues to this very day in many diverse ways, especially in seminaries and theology schools — all dominated by the Euro-American (especially Germanic) worldview and thus in perfect continuity with the conquering and crushing force of the first conquistadors of New Spain or the pilgrim fathers of New England. The poor native is still being denied the right to existence by the very missionaries who want to offer them salvation.[24]

This contradiction was the most regrettable error of the Span-

---

22. Orlando Espín, "Trinitarian Monotheism and the Birth of Popular Catholicism," *Missiology* 20, no. 2 (1992): 187.

23. Aquino, *Our Cry for Life*, 47.

24. It seems the only ones who are breaking from this Euro-American prohibition are some Pentecostals, since African-Mexican Pentecostalism is the only branch of Christianity that originated from among the ranks of the marginated and segregated poor of the Americas. See Harvey Cox, *Fire from Heaven* (New York: Free Press,

ish missionary effort and is the most profound error of today's
Western-dominated churches. It was (and is) so serious that some
have questioned the validity of the Mexican church (and the entire Latin American church), arguing that the exclusion of native
priests meant the entire endeavor was flawed from the very beginning.[25] For the most part, Indians, Africans, mestizos, and mulattos
are still excluded today from the Catholic priesthood, and even
more so the hierarchy. There is still a systematic exclusion of the
non-Western "colored" poor from ministry, priesthood, academia,
and religious life. This has been one of the great mortal sins of
our church that persists to our own day. No wonder Pentecostalism, which invites the poorest of the poor to minister and proclaim
the word of God without any humanly designed qualification, is
flourishing among the poor of the world.

At Tepeyac, Juan Diego functions as the priest. He responds
to the divine call and climbs the hill to be the mediator between
the Mother of God and the bishop, between his people and the
powerful people from Europe. He will now be her trusted messenger. In her presence, ordination is not necessary, for her recognition
and personal call constitute the basis of his apostolic mandate. It
is clear why the missioners, especially right after the Guadalupe
events, were so vehemently opposed to the growing and expanding Guadalupe tradition. They fully understood its theological and
ecclesial implications. This is probably one of the reasons for the
violent antinative feelings that grew among the missioners as the
Guadalupe tradition was being transmitted.[26] The call of Juan
Diego is a divine protest against the elitist policies of a church that
refuses to recognize the giftedness of the poor and lowly, especially
the non-Western ones.

No wonder, as Bishop Richard Ramírez has stated, that the
poor have shortcuts to God that the church has not yet discov-
ered. Indeed, the Mother of God, who is also the Mother of the
Church, established the very first of these shortcuts to God: her-

---

1995). I am beginning to wonder if Juan Diego was not the first Christian of the
Americas to undergo a Pentecostal experience and mission.

25. Ricard, *The Spiritual Conquest of Mexico,* 229.

26. Ricard, *The Spiritual Conquest of Mexico,* 35.

self, easily accessible to all. Even today, the more complicated and rule-oriented the church becomes, the more people go directly to God through La Morenita. The church is so complex, but she is so simple.[27] The church often keeps non–Euro-Americans away and reminds them of their Western-imposed sociocultural and racial inferiority while, at the same time, proclaiming their unquestioned dignity and nobility. Pope John Paul II proclaims loudly and prophetically the dignity and rights of the indigenous poor of the world, yet the very structures of the church he heads constantly impede these teachings from becoming a reality. No wonder the institutional church continues to lose credibility while Our Lady of Guadalupe continues to gain credibility.

Tepeyac is the site of several important contrasts: between the feminine aspect of God revered by the Indians and the European God as male; between being at home and being a foreigner and stranger in one's own land; between an enjoyable evangelization and a forced and painful one; between evangelization as dialogue and evangelization as didactic teaching; between the native priestliness of the people and an ordained foreign clergy; between personal transformation through God's grace and human victimization and sacrifices (of Indians, Spaniards, or anyone else).

Mount Tepeyac takes its place among the famous mountains of God's saving history. It is the Mount Sinai of the Americas, for it is here that God gives the new law of love, protection, and compassion for the people. It is the Mount of the Beatitudes of the Americas, for through the relationship and conversation between the Lady and Juan Diego, we can hear and experience a blessing pronounced on the poor, the meek, the lowly, the sorrowing, the peacemakers, and the persecuted of the New World. It is the Mountain of the Transfiguration of the Americas, for here the glory of God is clearly manifested to God's chosen one, Juan Diego. It is the Americas' version of the mountain from which the resurrected Lord commissioned the apostles to go forth and make disciples of all nations (Matt. 28:16), for it is here that Juan Diego

---

27. Jeanette Rodríguez, *Our Lady of Guadalupe: Faith and Empowerment among Mexican-American Women* (Austin: University of Texas Press, 1993).

is commissioned to go and request a common home for "all the inhabitants of these lands." It is indeed God's sacred mountain of the Americas.

Principal Protagonists

First she allowed herself to be seen by a poor and dignified person whose name is Juan Diego; and then her precious image appeared in the presence of the new bishop D. Fray Juan de Zumárraga. (v. 2)

The two Juans are the main witnesses of the miracles and the principal protagonists of the story. One saw her, conversed with her, and became her trusted messenger. The other, the official authority representing ultimate truth, converted to her upon receiving the sign that he had demanded. Who were these two men, and why is their social, cultural, and religious identity so crucial for the proper understanding of the universal implications of the Guadalupe event? I will purposely try to bring out the contrast between the two men, between the groups and social statuses that they represent. Although great tensions are evident throughout the narrative (similar to the tensions between certain persons and groups in the Gospels), there is no outright opposition between the two men, although there will be a certain amount of reversal of roles leading to a new mutuality and a new and unsuspected church.

Juan Diego: A Simple and Dignified Indian Campesino

Juan Diego is the first person we meet in the narrative, and throughout the Guadalupe adventure, he continues to be the main protagonist. There is no doubt that he was an Indian, and we know only too well how the Indians were regarded by the conquering Europeans: as barely human, at best.

The narrative is not content with telling us just that Juan Diego was an Indian — even though that alone would have placed him among the humiliated and oppressed mass of conquered peoples.

Indeed, the narrative tells us much more about the actual identity and status of this man who was about to become one of the most influential and well-known persons in the history of the Americas. Who is Juan Diego?

It was said that his home was in Cuauhtitlán. (v. 5)

Where we come from tends to say a lot about who we are. Cities, regions, and nations can stamp a certain personality on people. The story very clearly emphasizes that Juan Diego came from Cuauhtitlán. What does this tell us about Juan Diego and about the inner meaning of the regenerating force of Guadalupe?

Cuauhtitlán was an ancient city that had come into being at the very origins of the Nahuatl culture and civilization. By 691 A.D. it was a well-organized city and even then was considered one of the most ancient cities in the Valley of Mexico. It had been conquered by various groups, but throughout the various conquests, it managed to maintain its continuity with the Nahuatl culture, somewhat absorbing the conquerors into its own culture, for even those who overpowered it physically recognized its cultural superiority. It was a well-known and peaceful center of agriculture, weaving, and pottery.

The Nahuatl glyph for Cuauhtitlán consisted of a tree (including its roots). From the branches hung the head of the goddess Tlazolteotl, the patroness of weavers. The city was made up of hard-working and honest people who owned small properties as families (not as private individuals) and worked on them diligently as farmers, weavers, and pottery workers. Their self-dignity and respect for one another came from their relationship and interdependence with the land, with one another, with their ancestors, and with their gods. They had no need for gold or the accumulation of wealth because they were satisfied with the simple product of their daily work.[28] When the need arose, they could also be fierce warriors and were known as distinguished fighters. To be from

---

28. Toribio de Motolinía, as quoted in H. McKennie Goodpasture, *Cross and Sword: An Eyewitness History of Christianity in Latin America* (Maryknoll, N.Y.: Orbis Books, 1989), 23.

Cuauhtitlán was to be from the noble order of the eagle,[29] and
the eagle was the symbol of the Sun, indicating that these noble
persons were messengers of the Sun. The narrative tells us that Juan Diego owned a home in Cuauhtitlán. This means his family, grandparents, and ancestors would
have lived there. Thus he was in continuity with the previous generations and even with the very origins of Nahuatl life itself. He
was well rooted in his portion of earth and in the human tradition
that had given him life and formed his character. Juan Diego was
connected to the Indians' most ancient and venerated tradition, a
simple, dignified, and honorable man who could be trusted without question. We might say that for his people, his very origins
were proof of his uncontested credentials.

In contrast with the Europeans, for whom dignity depended on
power, wealth, and social status, for the Nahuatls dignity came
from the ability to work the land and to live in harmony with
others and in accordance with the ways of the elders. The gods had
created man and woman to work the earth the Lord and Lady of
creation had created for them: "He was created to till the soil and
she to spin and weave, that they give birth to other *macehuales* and
that they always work and never remain idle."[30] The poorest of the
poor could be even more dignified than the powerful and wealthy
who had removed themselves from working the earth.

But the text is also very careful to tell us several times that Juan
Diego was a *macehual/tzintli* (I have added the slash), that is, a
low-class but dignified laborer who did the basic work of society.
The term *macehual* had a complex history. Before the arrival of
the Aztecs, the word seems to have been used to designate common laborers, but the word also connoted simplicity and dignity.
By the time of the Aztecs, a hierarchy of priests, soldiers, and mer-
chants had developed, and the positive connotations of the term
seem to have slipped from it. For the Spaniards (after an initial period in which they had somewhat recognized the Indian nobility),
all Indians, even the nobility, became *macehuales* (with no positive

29. Alberto Fragoso Castanares, "Vida del Beato Juan Diego," *Histórica: Organo
del Centro de Estudios Guadalupanos*, no. 2 (June 1991).
30. León-Portilla, *Aztec Thought and Culture*, 106–7.

connotations), and they were treated as such. For the Spaniards, then, the word referred to the masses of Indian poor — the faceless and nameless of society, the ones who appear to be absent from human history. Only the Spaniards were señores, the visible and named landowners, while all the natives were relegated to an inferior and nameless social status. Thus, regardless of what his people considered him, Juan Diego was a *macehual* for the Spaniards.

The narrative recognizes this social reality but adds *tzintli* to *macehual*. The former means "dignified." It emphasizes that although in the eyes of some Juan Diego was only a *macehual* (no positive connotations), he was in his innermost essence a dignified human being made in the image and likeness of God. Regardless of what human forces have done to him and his people, he is the dignified person God created him to be. By uniting these two meanings into one identifying term, *macehual tzintli,* the narrative connects us to the origins of humanity according to the Nahuatl myths, the original dignity of men and women as townspeople, as people connected to one another, to the ancestors, to the earth, and to God.

Juan Diego is simple, unassuming, and down-to-earth. He appears to be one of the millions of faceless and powerless disinherited people of the land, one of the conquered people denied dignity or respectable social status by those in authority. He stands in sharp contrast to the newly arrived Spaniards who had quickly installed themselves as the lords and masters of their conquered subjects. Hernán Cortés had fought with unquestioned confidence in his military invincibility as God's chosen one: "Because we have the banner of the Cross, . . . God gave us this victory in which we killed many people."[31] According to the Europeans' diaries and commentaries of this period, God was pleased and glorified by the massive killings of the natives.

Power and might appeared as the signs of God's election. Some of the Spaniards even looked upon Cortés as the new Moses and as the providential person chosen by God to open the gates for

---

31. Quoted in Luis N. Rivera Pagán, "Conquest and Colonization: The Problem of America," *Apuntes* 12, no. 2 (1992): 47.

evangelization to take place. The missioners would then follow as
the living icons of God the Father, who was the source of all power
and might.[32] To them, the natives were intended by God to be their
natural servants, for even if they were human, they appeared as
underdeveloped children — minors who needed to be disciplined,
corrected, and controlled by the missioners or the *encomenderos*.[33]

   Cortés and his men were proud and righteous about their conquest. They were convinced God was on their side and were sure of
their cultural, biological, and religious superiority. Even the most
humble of the missioners were proud of their Christian identity and
dignity in contrast to the "poor unfortunate creatures" they were
trying to evangelize and civilize. The Spanish thought of themselves
as sent by God to chastise the Indians for their sins and the sins of
their ancestors. To punish the Indians was viewed as a great virtue.
Cortés would extol his violent conquest of Tenochtitlán as "the
most pious and elevated deed initiated since the conversion of the
Apostles."[34]

   She said: "Listen, my most abandoned son, dignified Juan:
   Where are you going?" (v. 20)

La Virgen recognizes this perverse condition and greets Juan Diego
with a dual greeting: "most abandoned son, dignified Juan," abandoned to abusive labor and nothingness by the authorities of the
new society but recognized as dignified by La Virgen. Juan Diego
stands for every person whose self-dignity has been crushed, whose
credibility has been destroyed, whose sense of worth has been
trampled. As he will tell us himself, he is nothing; he is a bunch
of dry leaves. He has been made to think of himself as excrement (v. 40). He no longer knows himself as he truly is, seeing
himself only through others' eyes as totally worthless and useless
(vv. 35–41).

   This is the most destructive element of oppression: the oppressed
cease believing in themselves and become convinced that only the

---

32. Espín, "Trinitarian Monotheism," 186–87.
33. *Encomenderos*: the ones to whom they had been commended for their care,
in effect, the ones to whom they had been given for forced labor.
34. Rivera Pagán, "Conquest and Colonization," 44.

oppressors can know and do things correctly. They become down-trodden and even ashamed of who they are. But La Virgen knows who he truly is and will reveal his true self to him: a self that is dignified, honored, and trustworthy. Here begins the gospel through Our Lady of Guadalupe. Here begins the revelation of the ultimate truth about the conquered Indians and all the crushed and downtrodden of the earth. What the world and even the church officials say about the Indians is false — the lies and blindness of the world — but what La Virgen recognizes and says is ultimate truth. It is the truth of Juan Diego himself.

Juan Diego as presented in the narrative brings out the contrast between the Indian as recognized by the Lady, who is the source of ultimate truth, and the Indian as judged by the Spaniards, who were so totally conditioned by their own cosmovision. At a time when the Indians' very humanity was being questioned and debated by the conquering Spaniards, the Lady affirms the fullness of their humanity and the dignity of their ancestors and their ways of life. As in New Testament times, God chooses to call the rejected, the ignorant, and the downtrodden of this world to be the agents of the new creation.

Juan de Zumárraga: The Bishop, Confident Messenger of God

> "Go there to the palace of the bishop of Mexico, and you will tell him in what way I have sent you as messenger." (v. 26)

This is quite a reversal of what had been happening. Juan Diego is told to go to the palace of the bishop. He is not to go there, however, to learn about the things of God; rather, he is to go to tell the chief spokesperson of God what to do. This was totally out of the ordinary. After all, the bishop had been zealous in telling the Indians about the falsity of all their notions of God, and now an Indian was to dare to go tell the bishop about the things of God. It seems absurd. Yet there is a deep, life-giving force in this apparent absurdity — typical of the foolishness and absurdity of the wisdom of God (1 Corinthians 1).

The palace of the bishop was both the real and the symbolic cen-

ter of the new evangelization and of the new socioreligious order
that were being imposed. It was the headquarters and command
post of those who presented themselves as the messengers of the
true God, the God who had overpowered the gods of the native
Mexicans. This was the ultimate center of the new civilization that
was being forced upon them. Here the Indians were not at home
and were not free to be the people God had made them to be. Yet
they could not ignore its presence. They could not undo what had
already become established. The obvious alternatives were either
to simply give into it and try to accommodate as well as possible
or to fight against it. Those certainly appeared to be the logical and
reasonable options, the options offered by the established ways of
thought, ways of thought that continue to this day. Could there
possibly be another way?

The palace is the place of the great masters; it is the place of
temporal and spatial power. It is the place of elegance, domination, intrigue, and servitude. It is the place where a few lord it
over the many, where no one is allowed to be truly human, for
all have to live out their expected and assigned roles. No one —
master or slave — is truly free or truly at home. It is a place of temporal grandeur and personal fear. From the palace proceeded all
the forces that would destroy the entire native way of life.

The bishop and his household were the ultimate authority of
the new social order. In the Christian cosmovision of that time,
the pope was the ultimate ruler of the universe, and the bishop in
the palace was the ultimate ruler of New Spain. It is true that he
was totally different from the conquistadors, but he was still one
of them. He and many other missioners had bitterly complained
against the abuses of the conquest, had defended the Indians, had
admired them in many ways, and had truly tried to Christianize
them in the best ways they knew, but ultimately, they had justified the established world order according to which the pope was
the ultimate authority of the world and the bishop was the ultimate authority in New Spain.[35] In and through the bishop of

35. Luis N. Rivera Pagán, *A Violent Evangelization* (Louisville: Westminster/John
Knox Press, 1992), 24–41.

New Spain, the all-powerful God appeared to approve and sanc-
tion the new world order that was now beginning to be built
from the very stones of the old. And in spite of the vigorous
complaints against the abuses, the missioners did not question the
validity of the authority of the new European-based world order
and cosmovision.

Fray Juan de Zumárraga was, along with many of the other
missioners, one of the greatest evangelizers and defenders of the
Indians. Yet he was equally one of the most fierce in destroying
anything that hinted of paganism. In one of his famous letters
(June 12, 1531), he wrote that he had destroyed more than five
hundred temples and twenty thousand idols.[36] He was convinced
that he first had to destroy before he could build the new church.
He was so busy destroying temples of the Indian deities, and then,
seemingly out of nowhere, this Indian, this *macehual,* wanted a
temple built at Tepeyac, the site of the ancient Indian goddess Tonantzin. How utterly ridiculous! I'm surprised he didn't have Juan
Diego flogged for such apparent nonsense.

The treatment of Juan Diego by the servants and confidants of
the bishop is typical of the treatment the poor still get today, not
just by the church but also by all the institutions and functionar-
ies of society: immigration officials, social security clerks, police,
schools, insurance companies, hospitals. . . . They are looked down
upon, made to wait, asked to come back another day after hours
of patient and silent waiting, treated harshly and without respect,
asked for more proof or references than anyone else.

> As soon as he [Juan Diego] arrived, he tried to see him [the
> lord bishop]. He begged his servants, his attendants, to go
> speak to him. After a long time, they came to call him, telling
> him that the lord bishop had ordered him to come in. As soon
> as he entered, he prostrated himself and then knelt. (v. 30)

When oppressed people are taken in as servants of the household
of the oppressors, some of them become especially vicious toward
their own people, lording their tiny bit of power over them. This is

---

36. Ricard, *The Spiritual Conquest of Mexico,* 37.

exactly what happened in New Spain: the Indian supervisors and then the mestizo supervisors became worse than the Spaniards in the treatment of the Indians. This continues to happen today in the southwestern United States, where Mexican-American bureaucrats treat the Mexican-American and Latin American poor worse than anyone else. They have interiorized the image of the cruel treatment of the poor as the way for good human beings to act. The assimilation of the evil ways of the oppressor by the oppressed is the worst result of oppression: the victim takes on the ways of life of the victimizer and begins to victimize others.

> *He left very saddened because in no way whatsoever had her message been accomplished. . . . [Juan Diego told Our Lady:] "By the way he [the lord bishop] answered me, as if his heart had not accepted it, [I know] he did not believe it. . . . Because in reality I am one of those campesinos, a piece of rope, a small ladder, the excrement of people . . ."* (vv. 33, 37, 40)

The treatment of Juan Diego by the household of the bishop makes him, and all his people who have been treated in a similar manner across the centuries, feel dirty, humiliated, ashamed, unworthy, inferior, and dumb. This is a horrible experience of the church, but unfortunately this is the experience of the church that many poor Indians, blacks, mestizos, and mulattos continue to have. In the church, where the white priests preside, the nonwhite is often made to feel nonhuman and is at best tolerated. To the degree that this domination is assimilated, the individual and collective self-destruction and self-alienation of the people increase, deepen, and produce a deep sense of existential shame. For the sake of salvation, the people are condemned to perpetual self-destruction. And worse yet, they are made to feel guilty. They are convinced that they are to blame for their lowliness:

> *"Forgive me, I will cause pain to your countenance and to your heart; I will displease you and fall under your wrath."* (v. 41)

The poor and oppressed are blamed for their own miserable situation. The victim is blamed by the victimizer, and thus the victimizer can appear as the saint and hero of society while condemning the victim to the status of public sinner. No wonder that today new independent churches with their own native ministers from among the ranks of the ordinary people and not controlled by European institutions are flourishing among the poor of the Americas — especially among the African, Latino, and Native peoples who have never been allowed to have their own as clergy or in positions of religious leadership.

In 1539, Indians, Africans, mestizos, and mulattos were officially denied ordination.[37] They could do the menial work for the white fathers, but they could never be called to ordination. Indeed, over the years many Mexican-American poor became lay brothers in the religious orders and congregations of the southwestern United States, but very few if any were invited to holy orders. Reasons were always found to tell us we were unfit, untrustworthy, and unworthy.

The church wanted us around to pay, pray, obey, and honor its prelates, but not to be equal partners, proclaim the word, and celebrate the sacrament. Thus, the very celebration of the Eucharist, over which only white priests presided for centuries, reinforced the destruction of the innermost self-dignity of the nonwhite peoples of the world and sacralized racial segregation. Unfortunately, God's sacrament of unity — the unity for which Jesus offered himself as victim on the cross — has functioned as the sign of ultimate division. Is this a living heresy of the church? Do sociological prejudices continue to negate the deepest and most beautiful doctrine of our faith — that through baptism we were all made brothers and sisters who are nourished with the eucharistic bread? Is this practice of exclusion from ordination an ongoing insult to the Eucharist itself?

Thus the palace of the bishop, the legitimizing center of the newly created world order, was at the source of a distinction that would plague the Americas for centuries to come: a distinction between whites, who would be considered as fully human, and nonwhites, who would be considered as a lesser humanity, as cre-

---

37. Ricard, *The Spiritual Conquest of Mexico*, 230.

ated by God to be the servants and slaves of the whites; between the European expression of the faith and the "pagan" ways of the natives. It is true that the church would invite everyone, would endure great struggles and sacrifices to preach the gospel and care for the poor and the sick, and would struggle to baptize everyone so that there would be a common space in which all could be and pray together. But within this sacred space of equality, there would be sharp racial-hierarchical divisions that would appear to have been established by the divine will itself. This would lead to a great ambiguity: while inviting everyone into the common household, the church sharpened the divisions within its household and sanctioned the radically unequal distribution of the goods of that household.

So the bishop and his household, on the one hand, and Juan Diego, on the other hand, present a sharp contrast between the all-powerful and the totally powerless; between the honored ones and the one without honor or dignity; between the arrogance of those in charge and the humility of the people; between the ultimate teacher and the supposedly know-nothing Indian; between institutional rejection and individual self-deprecation. Unfortunately, the palace of the bishop emerges as the place where the unworthiness of the Indian is legitimized and confirmed. Here, Juan Diego experiences his worthlessness, his nothingness. Is this not the effect that many churches, rectories, convents, schools, and chanceries still have on the poor?

Yet it is to these very places that the poor are sent as trusted messengers of God's love and compassion, to call the church forth to its original purpose: to be among the poor, the suffering, the afflicted, the rejected, the hurting, the untouchable..., so as to bring the healing and life-giving presence of God to all, especially to those in greatest need. To remain faithful to the ways of its founder, the church must always be in a process of renewal and reformation, and there is no one better than the poor and rejected of any age and place to challenge the church to this faithfulness.

It is through the poor that God constantly evangelizes the church, and in coming to them and settling among them, that church in turn evangelizes them and enriches them with new life.

Without the constant challenge of the poor, who do not feel at home in fancy and orderly church buildings, the church degenerates into mere ecclesial bureaucracy and empty rituals, but without the church, the poor easily degenerate through cruelty, harshness, self-pity, anxiety, petty politics, divisions, and nothingness.

It is the poor and rejected who keep the church from becoming so comfortably installed in this world that it forgets that it is to be in the world but not of it, that its very mission is to constantly challenge unto new life until the final consummation of time. Juan Diego is sent to the palace of the bishop to call the church, through the person of the bishop, to conversion, relocation, and new life. He does not go to condemn, insult, and castigate, but to invite and offer new possibilities of life. He does not threaten to build a different church but dares to call the highest authorities in the church to alter their ways — their carefully elaborated pastoral and liturgical plans — so as to be ever more faithful to the gospel and to the people they are called to serve. It is at the very core of the new civilization — the palace of the bishop — that the evangelical purification must begin and from there flow to the whole church and society, and it is the poor and the rejected who initiate this ongoing conversion of the church.

The singing that initiates the rehabilitation of Juan Diego at Tepeyac is like the announcement of the first dawn of new relationships, like the first tiny buds of the new spring. The dawn of the new creation begins with the empowerment of the crushed of the world. This is the sunrise that promises new life to the poor, the marginated, and the suffering. The early morning dawn announced the daybreak of the new creation.

– 3 –

Exquisite Flowers

Desert hill of Tepeyac, December 12, 1531:

> ...all kinds of exquisite flowers from Castile, open and flowering. (v. 81)

With the very first appearance of the Virgin, everything begins to change; everything is transformed; everything takes on a new look. Like the first buds of a new spring, initiating a new cycle of life, her presence will produce a new, beautiful, and exquisite flowering upon earth.

In her presence, Juan Diego experiences a new sense of being while all the things on the barren desert hill take on a new appearance: the rocks appear like emeralds and other precious stones; the earth shines like the rainbow; the cacti and other brush looked like the beautiful feathers of the precious birds; and the leaves and even the thorns of the trees seem to be made of gold (v. 18). In her presence, everything takes on a new light and fragrance. The innermost beauty and dignity of all creation become manifest in her presence. What is happening? What is she capable of bringing about?

Virgin and Mother

> He saw a lady who was standing and who was calling him to come closer to her side.... He marveled at her perfect beauty. ...Her clothing appeared like the sun, and it gave forth rays. (vv. 15–17)

Who is La Virgen for Juan Diego and subsequently for the millions of people across the ages, the Americas, and the oceans who have looked upon her merciful presence? The answers are too many and varied to deal with them here. We can begin to explore the matter, however, by examining how she first appears and how she introduces herself.

The Voice of the Virgin Heard by Juan Diego

> ... "*Dignified Juan, dignified Juan Diego.*" (v. 13)

The very sound of the voice of a person reveals much about that person and her or his mood in relation to us — anger, arrogance, righteousness, authority, fear, indifference, concern, doubt, confidence, friendship, peace, tranquillity...Humans communicate not just through words but also through the way they say those words. The very manner in which we speak to people reveals our inner attitude toward them and allows them to experience proximity or distance, concern or burden, familiarity or contempt, confidence or distrust, and many other attitudes. The very tone of voice communicates the position of the heart while the way in which we address them indicates what we think of them: friend, parent, superior, servant, and so on.

The first revelation of La Virgen's identity comes through the very way she addresses Juan Diego — she is one who provokes intimacy and affection. There is no indication in the narrative that Juan Diego was in any way fearful when he first heard her call. The natural anxiety that such an exceptional experience would produce is immediately calmed by the reassuring tenderness of her voice. Her voice is affirming, compassionate, and inviting. In her presence, there is no fear (v. 14). Quite the contrary, there is immediate acceptance and familiarity. Juan Diego is addressed not as *Indio* or with the generic *tu* (you) but by name. Rather than being put down, he is dignified by the very way in which he is addressed. There is no command issued, only an invitation offered. Furthermore, his name is uttered with the greatest respect, familiarity, and affection. He is being treated not as a child (as the missioners treated the Indians) but as a full and mature human being. This mirrors the manner of the presence of Jesus among the poor and marginated masses of his time.

> *He ... heard her thought and word, which were exceedingly re-creative, very ennobling, alluring, producing love.* (v. 19)

By her very voice, she lets us know that in her presence, we have nothing to fear; we have nothing to be ashamed of; we have nothing to worry about — for she knows us well, and she calls us by name to come to her side that she might be our faithful and loving companion. Her identity is brought out in her very first greeting and then throughout her ongoing conversations with Juan Diego. She will be our constant companion throughout the tribulations of life, giving life to our struggles and comfort in our tribulations.

But this Lady who is calling Juan by name in a very respectful and loving way is not just any ordinary person — Spaniard or Indian. Everything about her reveals her very special nature and identity.

The Virgin Seen by Juan Diego

> *He marveled at her perfect beauty. Her clothing appeared like the sun, and it gave forth rays.* (vv. 16–17)

Juan Diego is fascinated by what he sees. She is of perfect beauty, and her clothes radiate like the sun — in fact, it seems the very sun radiates out of her (vv. 15–17). No wonder he thinks he might be in heaven, the source of life and light. She is both radically unlike the Indian divinities (e.g., she is not distant and unapproachable, as the human-god Montezuma had been) and yet similar to them in some ways. The sun was the Nahuatl symbol of God, the God through whom one lives and is maintained in existence. But she is even greater than their God, for she covers the sun, while not extinguishing it; she stands upon the moon (the other manifestation of the deity) but does not crush it; so she will tell the Indians (and us) something beautiful and unsuspected about God (like Paul at the Areopagus [Acts 17:16–34], who tells the Greeks about their

unknown God); she will tell them and the church more about God than they had known or suspected. She does not destroy the natives' gods nor deny the God of Christians but presents something much more attractive and humanizing — both to the Indians and to the Christians of that moment of history and even today. She does not look like any of the natives' gods: she is so human, yet she radiates divinity. This was a great and startling mystery — so totally human and yet so evidently divine.

The missioners wanted to destroy the Indians' sacred statues and replace them with Euro-Christian imagery. She offers something totally new and inclusive of the statues of the natives and the images of the Christians. She is no mere Indian statue nor Christian image, for she has a pleasant voice that speaks the very language of the people. Even more, she has a compassionate face and beautiful eyes in which Juan Diego could see himself reflected in a loving, respected, and accepted way. She speaks their language and looks upon them with love, understanding, and compassion. The beauty and perfection of her eyes continue to fascinate scholars to this day.[1]

Her very presence brings about the experience of God. She is of the divine order but is also simple and unassuming. She does not provoke terror or anxiety, only comfort and joy. Because of her appearance, there is no doubt that she is of the highest nobility, but she does not sit on a throne or stool as, respectively, the Spanish or Indian nobility often did when presiding over their subjects. There are no pretenses of superiority, she simply wants to be among her people. She simply stands before Juan Diego as an equal, invites him to her side, and initiates the conversation in a very friendly and egalitarian way.

---

1. Dr. Gilberto Aguirre, a famous Texas ophthalmologist, in a conference on Our Lady of Guadalupe at the Mexican American Cultural Center in November 1995, stated: "It is inconceivable that in 1531 any artist, not even Michelangelo, could have had the presence of mind and acute observation to paint the reflections of those persons present in the bishop's room in the eyes of the Blessed Virgin. This could not possibly be the work of human hands." See also Carlos Salinas and Manuel de la Mora, *Descubrimiento de un busto humano en los ojos de la Virgen de Guadalupe* (Mexico City: Editorial Tradición, 1980).

When Juan Diego sees her for the first time, she is divinely beautiful and definitely one of his own brown-skinned, brown-eyed, and black-haired people. She is of the highest nobility, but she comes out of the very earth of the native peoples. In her, heaven and earth are once again in harmony. The floral imagery on her dress is typical of Indian decoration and symbolic of the interconnectedness of all creation. Her face, her features, and her dress are proper to an Indian woman at that time who was with child.[2] The glyph of the Aztec calendar right over her womb indicates that she is the mother of the baby Sun, the mother of the new life about to be inaugurated upon these lands. Her own words will bring this out when she tells Juan Diego that she will be the mother of all the inhabitants of these lands.

We speak about Guadalupe as an apparition, but it is really much more of an *encuentro,* a coming together of two friends. It is analogous to the encounter-appearances of the Risen Lord with his apostles. This is a person-to-person conversation, something quite different from the dealings the Indians had with the friars, which were definitely between the inferior student and the superior teacher. Juan has not worked for this gift. It is a gratuitous gift from God, and Juan responds enthusiastically. In a manner typical of the great prophets of Israel, Juan does not consider himself worthy of the gift. But like the prophets he is obedient to the call, even after being rejected by the high and mighty: if God calls, Juan, like the prophets, will go ahead with his mission no matter the consequences.[3]

Juan Diego treats the Lady with great respect but also with great familiarity. He calls her *"niña mía"* (my daughter). When he is rejected, he knows that she too has been rejected and therefore calls her *"la mas desamparada"* (the most abandoned [v. 35]), as she had called him. She appears as the Indian Mother of God and the abandoned mestizo child of the Indian people. Through her, God

2. Salvador Pallares, "La aparición de la Virgen de Guadalupe," *Servir* 17, nos. 93–94 (1981): 252–53; and Gabriel Mauricio y Jiménez, "La santa imagen del Tepeyac: Lo que ahí está y no hemos visto," *Histórica: Organo del Centro de Estudios Guadalupanos,* no. 1 (March 1991).

3. Pallares, "La aparición de la Virgen de Guadalupe," 252–53.

vindicates the downtrodden. In her, the Indians and their ancestors are vindicated. Through her, a new means of evangelization — purified of ethnocentric limitations — is suggested. She inaugurates a counter to the spiritual conquest of the Indians. The conquered will triumph, but not through the ways of violence and threats of hell.

Her Self-Introduction

"I am the Ever-Virgin Holy Mary, Mother of the God of Great Truth, Téotl, of the One through Whom We Live, the Creator of Persons, the Owner of What Is Near and Together, of the Lord of Heaven and Earth." (v. 22)

She introduces herself as the Ever-Virgin Holy Mary. One of the most devastating insults of the conquest had been the rape of the native women, the abandonment of the mestizo children who were the offspring of the rapes, and the castrating effect this had on the Indian men who were forced to witness the rape of their own beloved and respected women but were not able to do anything about it. Here begins the great existential shame of the Latin American *raza* (race).[4] The type of sexual abuse and promiscuity demonstrated by the Spaniards — which was typical of the Renaissance life of Europe — had been unheard of in pre-Columbian America.[5] These acts by the Spaniards are at the root of one of the most shameful characteristics of Latin American life: abused women, psychologically castrated men, and abandoned children.[6]

The Lady is not just a virgin: she is Holy Mary, the one who could perfectly understand the pain, the agony, and the shame of the moment, for in her earthly existence as Mary of Nazareth, as the mother of a child with no identifiable human father, she par-

---

4. See Darcy Ribiero, "The Latin American People," in *1492–1992: The Voice of the Victims,* ed. Leonardo Boff and Virgil Elizondo (London: SCM Press, 1990); Octavio Paz, *The Labyrinth of Solitude* (New York: Grove Press, 1961); and Magnus Morner, *Race Mixture in Latin America* (Boston: Little, Brown & Co., 1967).

5. José Antonio Maravall, *El mundo social de "La Celestina"* (Madrid: Editorial Gredos, 1972).

6. María Pilar Aquino, *Our Cry for Life: A Feminist Theology from Latin America* (Maryknoll, N.Y.: Orbis Books, 1993), 43–48.

ticipated personally and intimately in the lot of the abused women and men of this world.[7] Even her saintly and just husband-to-be had decided to abandon her. The world of her time would consider her soiled, but God would maintain her virginal, and henceforth all generations would call her blessed, and her "fatherless" child would be the Lord and savior of humanity.

The Ever-Virgin Holy Mary now takes on the flesh of the Indian women of the Americas. She comes to the Americas in the form and figure, in the countenance and heart, of La Morenita del Tepeyac. Here now is one of their own, pregnant with new life and untouched by abusive hands. Her virginity is not in opposition to human conjugal relations but is a repudiation of one of the worst effects of the conquest: the rape of the women and the abandonment of both women and children by the abusing fathers. In her, both women and men humiliated by the Spanish rape are rehabilitated, for God maintains in virginal purity what sinful men and women violate and cast away as soiled. Her virginity is a sign of the human integrity of those who have been raped and humiliated.[8] La Virgen is not against sex; she is against domination through the sexual violation of the defenseless. Because she is one of the violated people, she can understand brokenness; because she is of God, she can completely rehabilitate those who have been abused.

Our Lady of Guadalupe goes on to further introduce herself as the Mother of the true God of the Christian Spaniards and equally the Mother of the God of the Nahuatls. She is the mother of both and as such is the mother of the new children of these lands. She is the mother of the new *mestizaje* of the Americas. In her we move from the radical opposition of the two religions to a new synthesis that will occur in the new life that she is about to give birth to — the new Christianity of the new humanity of the Americas. She will be the compassionate and listening mother of all who come to her.

---

7. Jane Schaberg, *The Illegitimacy of Jesus: A Feminist Theological Interpretation of the Infancy Narratives* (San Francisco: Harper & Row, 1987).

8. John Paul II, July 10, 1996, General Audience: "While the church's teaching does not define the term 'virgin,' the normal meaning would be assumed: that of the voluntary abstention from sexual acts and the preservation of physical wholeness." Thus the women who were abused against their will remained virgins and in physical wholeness. They are the virgin mothers of the Americas.

There is a very interesting gradual evolution in the presentation
of La Virgen. First she introduces herself as the Mother of God —
the God of the Spaniards, the God of the ancient Nahuatl tradition — and the mother of all the inhabitants of the land. Then
Juan Diego sees her as the mother of Jesus. She never tells him that
she is the mother of Jesus, but Juan Diego recognizes her as such.
This is probably the first theological reflection (versus simple memorization) of the Americas, for Juan Diego combines what he has
learned from the friars about Jesus Christ with what he has heard
and seen at Tepeyac and deduces that she is the mother of our Lord
and Savior Jesus Christ.[9] Finally, La Virgen presents herself as the
very personal mother of Juan Diego — she is not just the mother of
all the poor and afflicted as a group but is the mother of each one
in a very personal way. When one witnesses the devotion of her
children, there is no doubt that they have understood this aspect of
the message very well. She is in every sense *"mi madrecita"* — my
very own loving mother.

Mother of Everyone

> *"I am your merciful mother and the mother of all the na-*
> *tions that live on this earth who would love me, who would*
> *speak with me, who would search for me, and who would*
> *place their confidence in me. There I will hear their laments*
> *and remedy and cure all their miseries, misfortunes, and*
> *sorrows."* (vv. 24–25)

Having clearly identified herself in every way as having divine authority and nobility, she now comes to the core of the revelation:
she wants to be the very personal mother of all the inhabitants of
"the nations." She is not just the mother of the gods of the Indians' ancestors or the Ever-Virgin Mary of the Christians but is also
the ever-present and listening mother of each and every inhabitant
of the nations. Everyone can come to her without fear or hesitation. She is here and will always be here to listen, comfort, console,
heal, and give life. She demands nothing of us; she asks only to be

---

9. Siller Acuña, *Para comprender el mensaje de María de Guadalupe*, 80.

ever-present to respond to our cries and lamentations and remedy our ills.

In many ways this is the most tender and personal passage of the account, and it is at the heart of what generations of devotees — beginning with Juan Diego and Juan Bernardino — have experienced. Her listening face and her healing abilities are among the most evident and immediate characteristics of her real love and presence among us. She will make our struggles her own — something she did during the Mexican War of Independence and for the Farm Workers' movement in the United States. Mexican tradition has it that after the invasion of the United States into Texas, California, and lands in between, she stopped the invasion at the Rio Grande. A new tradition maintains that she will find ways of breaking the electronic curtain that keeps the poor of Latin America from migrating into the United States and of uplifting the Indians of Chiapas and throughout the Americas to obtain their legitimate rights and place throughout these lands.

Many titles have been given to her over the ages, but I do not know of any that is uttered more universally and with greater love and confidence than "Madrecita Querida" (Beloved Mother). Regardless of how theologians and dogmaticians explain it, for the people at large, she is the beloved maternal presence of God.

Contrasts

The contrasts are quite startling. She is not concerned with idols or demonic presence. She comes not to destroy anyone or anything but to bring to perfection the ways of the ancestors and to purify and correct the ways of the Christians. She has no weapons, only a friendly and alluring presence. She does not ask for the sacrifice of anyone or that anyone be punished for not accepting her invitation. She is one of the people, yet noble and regal in presence. She has withstood the conquest and remained unsoiled and unbroken; she is neither the cruel and dominating Spaniard nor the defeated, shamed, and crushed Indian; she is, rather, the ever-virgin mother of new life. She will invite all who come to her to a new vision of themselves and of one another.

La Virgen is a beautiful woman who captures our hearts with love, a child of the land, a companion of the suffering and marginated, a caring and compassionate mother, mother of the Creator and Redeemer, mother of all the inhabitants of this land, mother of the new humanity, the feminine heart and face of God.

Her Temple: Sacred Space

"I very much want and ardently desire that my hermitage be erected in this place. In it I will show and give to all people all my love, my compassion, my help, and my protection, because I am your merciful mother and the mother of all the nations that live on this earth who would love me, who would speak with me, who would search for me, and who would place their confidence in me. There I will hear their laments and remedy and cure all their miseries, misfortunes, and sorrows.

"And for this merciful wish of mine to be realized, go there to the palace of the bishop of Mexico, and you will tell him in what way I have sent you as messenger, so that you may make known to him how I very much desire that he build me a home right here, that he may erect my temple on the plain. You will tell him carefully everything you have seen and admired and heard." (vv. 23–26)

Telling the bishop to go build the church at Tepeyac — a place away from Mexico City — was somewhat like the Risen Lord telling the disciples to go to Galilee, where they would see him. The gospel continues to break down all barriers, especially the religious idols of any religion, in places that are away from the great centers of power and glory. The kingdom of God's universal love among all men and women is inaugurated on the margins. It is in the barrios, the migrant camps, and storefront churches that the Risen Lord continues to appear.

The Spanish missioners were very busy burning Indian temples and building Christian temples all over New Spain. Why would the

Lady from Heaven want another temple? Wouldn't the missioners be totally opposed to this — a temple requested by an Indian in the name of some sort of Indian divinity, one from Tepeyac (the old sanctuary of Tonantzin) who identified herself with the gods of the Indians' ancestors? It is certainly easy and logical to understand the hesitation of the bishop and his entire household.

The natives went to the Spanish temples to hear how bad and sinful their people had been and how they had to convert or be damned for all eternity. They heard how the Spanish had been sent by God to punish them for their sins. The cruelty of the Spaniards was necessary because their sins and those of their ancestors had been so profound. They were constantly told that the Spanish were God's instruments to punish them for their sins and save them from hell. In Spanish temples, they were put down by the priests, the living icons of God the Father; in the hermitage at Tepeyac they would be uplifted by the Mother of God. The fathers told the Indians about hell and damnation; the Mother offered protection and comfort. The fathers spoke about the hereafter; she spoke about the here and now. The fathers spoke and the Indians listened; she wanted to listen to all those who cry and suffer in silence. The fathers had many rules and doctrines; the Mother had simple love and compassion. In her temple, all would be equally welcomed without distinction.

In La Virgen's temple, anyone — first the Indians and then everyone else — would be able to converse freely with the Mother, a close friend and a caring relative. There would be give and take. In the Spanish temples, the friars perpetuated the superior-inferior relationship that had been established by the conquest and even argued that it could not be otherwise.[10] In fact, they would make this superior-inferior relationship appear to be of divine order and thus established for all eternity. This is definitely not the kind of temple and relationship the Lady is asking for. The type of relationship perpetuated in the Spanish temples and in the centers of power was the counterside of the kingdom of God as lived and

---

10. Robert Ricard, *The Spiritual Conquest of Mexico: The Evangelizing Methods of the Mendicant Orders in New Spain, 1523–1572,* trans. Lesley Byrd Simpson (Berkeley: University of California Press, 1966), 224–35.

proclaimed by Jesus. That is why the Lady wanted her temple built away from the new center of civil-religious power in Mexico City and among the people at Tepeyac.

The Mother of God wants a home where all will be welcomed, where all who come will receive her recognition, love, and affection. Here, everyone will be heard; all will be free to speak in their own way. Her very eyes show that she recognizes the presence of the one who comes to her. Her very gaze lets those who are looking at her know she is ready and willing to listen to them. She is not cold, distant, and haughty, but tender, close, and friendly. She does not want her children threatened; she wants them protected. She does not want them humbled and dehumanized; she wants them self-confident and joyful.

Her house is to become what every church should be: a center of recognition, listening, love, compassion, healing, and protection. This will be a center not of rules and regulations but of flowers and songs. It will not be a sad church, but a festive one wherein the joy of God will uplift the downtrodden of the earth.[11] The humanizing and liberating beauty of the divine experience will draw people into it freely and joyfully. Here, everyone will be someone special, experiencing their inner dignity, infinite worth, and personal mission of building the temple of the new and truly egalitarian society. This is what every church should be. So her temple is to be a model of what every Christian temple should be, a model that few, even today, emulate.

Because she is the Mother of the Church, she wants the church unified. She does not want the new church to be separated from the established church, so she sends Juan Diego to invite the bishop to enter into her project for the new and true church of the Americas.

---

11. One of the main objections of the Indians to the Christian religion was that it was devoid of all joy and happiness. The missioners seemed opposed to all happiness on earth and to anything that gave pleasure. Theirs was a religion of sadness and punishment. In the words of a prominent elder of Tlaxcala: "These poor fellows [the missioners] must be sick or must be crazy.... Without a doubt it must be a great pain that they carry because they are men without sense, since they neither search out pleasure nor joy but rather sadness and solitude." From Camargo's *Historia de Tlaxcala*, as quoted in Miguel León-Portilla, *Endangered Cultures* (Dallas: Southern Methodist University Press, 1990), 75.

It would not be separate from the church of the living Christian tradition, but it would begin the renewal and reform of the whole church that the old church of Europe was no longer capable of initiating, even though it would keep on trying even to our day.

So the Virgin Mother is asking not just for a building but also for a way of being church that is truly in conformity with the Christian communities and churches of the early apostolic movement. She anticipates the ecclesiology of Vatican II by more than four hundred years, but then the mother of Jesus was always ahead of others in anticipating people's needs, as was evidenced at Cana of Galilee. The temple of Tepeyac would be sacred space precisely because everyone would be welcomed there, and it would help sacralize the Americas by being a place and model for breaking down all barriers of separation — even national and racial boundaries — so that no one would be excluded, marginated, or deprived in these lands. She is, indeed, the one mother *"of all the nations that live on this land."*

The New Cosmic Life

Health: Healing

They saw his uncle, who was well and with no pains. (v. 114)

Healing was the great gift of Jesus, and it continues to be a great gift today. Certainly science has come a long way in healing arts and techniques, yet many still believe — based on many personal testimonies — in the power of God to heal. There is no doubt that the main reason for the spread of the love for and devotion to Our Lady of Guadalupe has been her reputation for healing — physical, psychological, spiritual, material. She is known as the very caring mother who is always there for us, especially in moments of need. As she was there for Juan Bernardino, she continues to be there for us today whenever we need her.

The sickness of Juan Bernardino was certainly very real in itself, but it was also representative of all the collective trauma, exhaustion, and incurable maladies — psychological, social, spiritual, and

physical — that had come with the conquest and that were destroying the various nations of Mexico. He is representative of all his
people who were dying because of the cruelty of the conquest, because of the loss of the desire to live, or as a consequence of the
new diseases that came with the European invaders.

The Euro-Christian religion, as presented by the priests, offered
salvation in the hereafter, but Our Lady, like Jesus, offers a foretaste of the afterlife by healing the sick in the here and now and
inviting everyone to forgiveness, reconciliation, sharing, concern,
and togetherness. The elements of the gospel that were missing
from the Christendom of that period are introduced into the New
World by the mother of the baby Son/Sun.

Her presence begins to reverse the devastation of the conquest —
the effects would not be immediate any more than the effects of the
death-resurrection of Jesus have been, but the Guadalupe events
would definitely mark the beginning of the new era, of the new
Sun who is the Son of God fully incarnated in the soil of the Americas. Juan Diego regains his self-dignity and confidence while Juan
Bernardino is healed and restored to life. The rehabilitation of the
dying uncle not only is the ultimate sign and proof of new life for
the dying peoples but is equally the beginning of a hope based
in the new healing, protective, and effective power now present
among them.

The healing power of Our Lady of Guadalupe that started with
Juan Bernardino continues today. Countless miracles have been attributed to her intercession.[12] I have heard of many of them, have
been told of many of them directly by people who experienced
them, and even have experienced some of them myself. The personal testimonies of the faithful are unlimited and ongoing. The
people tell one another about these miracles. It is the people who
continue to transmit the tradition that in turn continues to bring
life and healing to them. They continue to bring flowers of thanks-
giving every day and everywhere there is an altar in her honor; they
compose songs about her and reproduce her image artistically — all

---

12. Ernesto de la Torre Villar and Ramiro Navarro de Anda, *Testimonios
históricos guadalupanos* (Mexico City: Fondo de Cultura Económica, 1982).

in deep gratitude for the favors, the healings, that she continues to bring about. These favored people need no explanation about her identity or mission; they know her to be the Mother of God and our mother who hears our laments and remedies our ills. There is no doubt about her existence.

It was Juan Bernardino, the first of millions to experience her healing power and give personal testimony of what she had done, who officially revealed what she wanted to be called: *"The Ever-Virgin Holy Mary of Guadalupe"* (v. 119).

Beauty: Beautiful Flowers out of Season

All over the place there were all kinds of exquisite flowers from Castile, open and flowering. It was not a place for flowers, and likewise it was the time when the ice hardens upon the earth. (v. 81)

The beautiful flowers that appeared on the cold morning of December 12 in the desert atop Mount Tepeyac were the sign chosen by the Lady so that Juan Diego would be believed. This sign would turn out to go beyond what the bishop had demanded. The flowers complete the divine revelation begun with the sign of music. The divine message is now brought to completion in the flowers picked, carried, and presented to the world by Juan Diego — the very one who had seemed to have nothing to offer but cheap labor. This was the final touch that assured the native people that what happened at Tepeyac was of God. God had spoken through flower and song. No question about it. And these same flowers were also to be the ultimate proof that would convert the bishop and his household so that they would believe Juan Diego and would thus carry out La Virgen's desire to build the new church of the Americas.

The ultimate proof was not the military might of God, as had been claimed by the missioners, but the attractive power of beauty, respect, and compassion. Truth does not reside in domination and power; in fact, domination and power are obstacles to truth. Might does not make right. Rather, it is through loving compassion and natural simple beauty that the glory of God's truth shines forth and is made evident for all to grasp. This is the truth of God, the truth of men and women, and the truth of life. Guadalupe is the truth of beauty and the beauty of truth — the beautiful truth of the single-hearted children of God who behold the face of God (Matt. 5:8). This is the ultimate truth of *flor y canto* (flower and song), the truth that is experienced through all the senses, through every fiber of one's being and in the deepest recesses of one's soul. The beautiful flowers that gave forth the heavenly perfume complete the revelation initiated by the singing of the birds. Now the truth of God is complete.

Evangelization through *flor y canto* contrasts sharply with the method of catechesis of that period, and in spite of all the obstacles, it is still the most effective means of evangelization and catechesis. The ultimate sign given by the missioners to the natives to convince them to believe in Christianity was the sword (today replaced by rules and regulations). After exposing all the beautiful things about Christianity, which the natives could not comprehend and if they could comprehend, could not accept as true, the missioners would remind the natives that the God of the Christians had overpowered their own gods in battles and therefore was the true God that the natives must believe in or perish. In contrast to this "sign of the sword," flowers are the sign given by the Lady for the bishop and the church. For the native world (which had not demanded any sign), the beautiful flowers, I repeat, complete the divine communication begun by the beautiful singing. For the church, the flowers are the absolute repudiation of evangelization by way of domination and severe punishment.

John Paul II has spoken about a new evangelization. It is my conviction that this new evangelization started with the Guadalupe event. The gospel will bear fruit not through threats, well-developed programs, formal catechisms, or dogmatic arguments that fail to communicate the transforming beauty and joy of the good news of God's universal love. The content may be wholly orthodox, but the medium is empty of life — like a fine, expensive, polished car without spark plugs or fuel. The gospel comes alive and is life-giving through the witness of personal understanding and compassion. The *flor y canto* of God's revelation today shine through brightly in the colorful and joyful fiestas of God's poor that invite all to join in without distinction — all are attracted, as Juan Diego was, to the beautiful music, to the spontaneous joy of these religious fiestas. Many of our modern programs give a lot of information but little or no experience of the divine. We speak a lot about God but do not lead people into a mystical experience of God like that which Juan Diego had at Tepeyac and millions continue to have today when they are alone or together in Our Lady's presence.

Friendship: Her Floral Image on the Tilma

In that very moment she painted herself: the precious image of the Ever-Virgin Holy Mary, Mother of the God Téotl, appeared suddenly, just as she is today and is kept in her precious home, in her hermitage of Tepeyac, which is called Guadalupe. (v. 107)

Beyond the *flor y canto* and beyond the sign asked for by the bishop, Our Lady leaves an additional gift: her living image miraculously painted on the cloth of Juan Diego's *tilma* (shoulder cape made of native cactus fiber). Many scientists have studied the *tilma*, and they say that there is no explanation for many of its qualities.[13] The cloth was not suitable for paintings; there are no brush marks; the cloth has not deteriorated. What Juan Diego saw in 1531 is here with us for all to see and appreciate, and through it Our Lady continues her conversation with us today. The image and the words together constitute a harmonious audiovisual poem: the image is the poem that can be seen, and the poem is the image that can be heard, and together they constitute one coherent divine manifestation.

It is difficult to explain the meaning of the *tilma* to someone who has not experienced it in the presence of the people. It is truly a living and enduring presence. It is like a collective womb that allows all who pass through it to be reborn into something new:

---

13. Jody Smith, *The Image of Guadalupe: Myth or Miracle?* (New York: Doubleday, 1984).

recognized, affirmed, dignified, family,...all children of the same Mother and united with the loving Father. This was my own personal experience the first time I went on pilgrimage with my father when I was a young boy. I felt I had entered into the very womb of earth out of which we as a people had been born. Beyond that, she is ever-present for us, ready to listen to our most intimate thoughts, wishes, and desires. Millions continue to have this experience with La Virgen.[14] She is not a distant deity but a close personal friend, a faithful companion, and a loving mother.

The image on the *tilma* reveals that Our Lady is of the highest nobility, for she is dressed in the blue-green of divinity. But it also reveals that she is of the earth, for her dress is the color of earth and is adorned with various floral arrangements, indicating the flourishing of the new humanity that she will bring about. This noble and exalted Lady is not an Indian god, for those gods created fear, while she has beautiful eyes that attract us to her. She is divine, yet she sees us as equals — she is not sitting (as a superior would) but is standing, calling the lowly to rise from their stooped humiliation. Her face radiates concern and compassion for all those in need. Her hands offer everything that she is to us. Her black band indicates that she is expectant of new life, and the glyph over her womb indicates that she carries within her the life of the baby Sun. In her, there is life, continuity, and transcendence; and most of all, there is hope for salvation here and now, today.

The most important and noble person to have come since the conquest (indeed, since the coming of her Son) does not allow her exalted status to keep her from entering into a close and intimate friendship with Juan Diego and everyone else, without exception. Through her presence on the *tilma,* she continues to make herself present to all who come to her.

---

14. For some excellent personal testimonies of this living phenomenon of friendship between Our Lady of Guadalupe and those who have faith in her, see Jeanette Rodríguez, *Our Lady of Guadalupe: Faith and Empowerment among Mexican-American Women* (Austin: University of Texas Press, 1993).

Part III

THE NEW CREATION

✳   ✳
   ✳

— 4 —

Conversion

*"Thus faith started; it gave its first buds; and it flow-
ered in the knowledge of the One through Whom
We Live, the true God, Téotl.* (v. 4)

The Great Equalizer

Our Lady is about the blossoming of Christian faith in the
Americas and can best be understood in the context of the very
first blossoming of the Christian faith among the earliest followers of the way of Jesus. The whole Christian movement, from the
earliest preaching of Jesus himself, is about repentance and conversion. There is no doubt that everyone is called to repent and
convert, but, practically speaking, conversion means totally different things to different people, depending on where they are within
sociocultural structures.

Jesus was most respectful and understanding with women, the
poor, the downtrodden, the public sinners, the prostitutes, the sick,
the ignorant, the aliens, the rejected, the small-time bureaucrats,
and the ordinary simple folk of the land. He called them to repent
from their inner feelings of worthlessness, inferiority, disgrace, and
shame caused by the socioreligious structures that had convinced
them of their sinful status. He called them to convert — have a
change of heart — so as to recognize themselves for what they truly
were: dignified children of God with unlimited potential for doing
good. Jesus was quick to pierce through the dehumanizing con-
victions, labels, and prejudices of society that condemn not only

individuals but entire groups — women, ethnic groups, races — to existential inferiority and shame. The sin of the world has created the sociocultural blindness that keeps us from appreciating the true beauty, dignity, and worth of individual persons and entire human groups. Jesus calls us to repent from the sinful (righteous and judgmental) way of viewing human beings and human groups and to convert to a new way of seeing ourselves and others — to see each other as God our Creator and loving Parent sees us.

Jesus is harsh in dealing with the righteous, the arrogant, the rich, and the mighty of his time — the apparently good and beautiful people of his own culture and religion who were convinced they had the monopoly on truth and holiness and had the physical means to impose their views on everyone else. The prophets before him had castigated their own people for their exploitation of the poor, the defenseless, the alien workers, the widows, the orphans, and the strangers. Jesus condemns the temple as a "den of thieves" because their religion of the covenant now served as a mask to hide and disguise their injustices, making the exploitation of the poor appear as a virtue of the people of God. What blasphemy. Jesus continues the denunciation begun by the prophets and is not afraid to call all persons, even the high priest, to accountability to the very foundations of the religion that they professed. He calls everyone to repentance and conversion, but, as is evident from the Gospels, it was quite difficult or even impossible for those who had vested interests to convert: those in authority, the righteous, the rich, and the powerful. They too were invited, but they had other things to do, other more pressing interests to protect.

If repentance and conversion were difficult for the righteous and the powerful in the time of Jesus, they would become even more difficult for the righteous and the powerful who were convinced they were already Christians, and this was even truer when the latter's Christian faith was convenient to justify their wealth-accumulating enterprises. They simply did not think of themselves as candidates for conversion. Until Vatican II, *Evangelii Nuntiandi* (the visionary and prophetic letter of Pope Paul VI), and the mounting call of Pope John Paul II to recognize the collective sins of the past of the so-called Christian peoples, Christian churches had not thought of their own need to convert. Conversion had been seen as a one-time thing — once one was a Christian, periodic confession and renewal were all one needed; one certainly did not need a radical conversion from one's so-called Christian way to the way of Jesus. Renewal of the church was part of a tradition that had given rise to many of today's religious communities, but that renewal was not thought of in terms of conversion.[1] Evangelical renewal inflamed and shaped the dreams of the first missioners to the Americas,[2] but they never thought in terms of the much more urgent need: the conversion of their own Euro-Christian church, civilization, culture, and cosmovision.

Paul VI was not afraid to call the church to conversion from the new idols that appear daily (*Evangelii Nuntiandi*, no. 15). But, like the Christians in the sixteenth century, many in the church continue to think only of taking the gospel to others, not of listening to it and being converted by it anew. Thus, then as now, the church creates new idols within itself while fanatically trying to destroy what it does not understand and sees as the idols of others. When we stop listening to the gospel each day, the conversion process stops for a person, a church, or a culture, and we will surely make of the social expressions of our religion a new and forceful idol that will keep us from growing and deepening in the following of Jesus.

Repentance and conversion are not simple matters and become most complicated when missioners accompany a conquering and dominating group, as in the case of the early European missioners who came to the Americas and today's European and American missioners who go to Third World countries. As a whole, the church of Jesus Christ has remained a European-American affair. Are the missioners agents of cultural domination or authentic witnesses of the gospel? Our answer is usually ambiguous, for the truth usually lies somewhere between these extremes. In fidelity

1. For a good discussion of the ongoing renewal of the church until the time of Vatican II, see Hans Küng, *The Council, Reform and Reunion* (New York: Sheed and Ward, 1961), 61–147.

2. Jacques Lafaye, *Quetzalcoatl and Guadalupe* (Chicago: University of Chicago Press, 1976), 303–6 and 139ff.; Casiano Floristán, "Evangelization of the 'New World': An Old World Perspective," *Missiology* 20, no. 2 (1992): 138–40.

to the mandate of Christ to go and make disciples of all nations, missioners have always been motivated by their sincere desire to convert nonbelievers to Christ, but what does conversion to Christ mean? Does it mean rejecting one's culture in favor of the culture of the missioners? Does it mean becoming ashamed of who one is for the sake of becoming a Euro-American? Is conversion a turning from one culture to another or a turning to a new way of living within one's own culture? Christianity is about conversion, but just what is conversion?

The happenings at Tepeyac and the story of Our Lady of Guadalupe have always been associated with the conversion of the Indians. In fact, some have claimed the church engineered the whole thing to manipulate the Indians. However, according to the earliest documentation, church officials tried to quash the phenomenon because they saw it as ruining their missionary efforts. They were trying to discredit and destroy the natives' ancient religious traditions, and Our Lady was bringing those traditions together with much of the imagery and message of the missioners. The missioners saw the phenomenon as an invention of the Indians to restore their ancient religions. If anything, they saw it as a major obstacle to conversion as they understood it.

The entire Guadalupe happening is about a multiplicity of forms of conversion, not simply about entry into the Catholic Church, which was how the missioners conceived of conversion. Guadalupe brought about conversion in ways that were desperately needed but that were not suspected by anyone at the time; in fact, it converted the very notion of conversion itself. The repentance and conversion dynamics of Guadalupe followed those of the gospel, thus purifying and correcting those of the militaristic, ethnocentric Christendom of that time.

Juan Diego and, subsequently, vast numbers of the native peoples easily and quickly accepted the authenticity and authority of the Lady and her message. In her presence, their fundamental dignity and infinite worth were experienced and affirmed. Henceforth, Indians would missionize one another in their own language and through their personal testimonies with or without the presence of the officials of the church. The millions of voluntary conversions that followed are proof of the response. The Indians' ongoing devotion to Christ through Our Lady of Guadalupe is evident and still growing to this day.

The faith of the poor and marginated is not superficial or simplistic, as is often claimed by the so-called experts in the faith — persons who are more expert in the intellectual form of Western religion than in the faith that resides in the hearts and illuminates the mind with new insight. Neither is it a pagan faith loaded with idols and superstitions, as is claimed by some Catholics, Protestants, fundamentalists, and Pentecostals. The simple, ordinary Christian faith of Latin Americans and of the Latinos/as in the United States is rooted not in the propositions of the faith or creeds or in the memorization of biblical texts but in the personal knowledge of Jesus, the Father as La Providencia, Mary as mother and comforter, and the saints as personal friends. It is through La Virgen that the people continue to be reborn into this new life of faith.

The early missioners were saintly men. They sincerely wanted to convert the natives so that they might be saved. But in order to convert, the Indians had to give up everything that had been of value to them before the Spanish arrival. The missioners were fed up with the corruption of European Christianity, but they were so obsessed with destroying anything that hinted at the diabolical and magical that they were unable to appreciate the many manifestations of grace and the seeds of the Word present in the native ways of life.[3] They saw and judged everything and anything that was strange or different in terms of the Old Testament's condemnation of idols, demons, and diabolical possession and manifestations. They were zealous in their mission to eradicate idolatry in every shape and form and to convert the natives to their religion. Because of the unity of the religion and civilization of Europe, the missioners could not distinguish between conversion to Jesus and conversion to the Spanish culture — they despised the corruption of Spanish culture but did not question the legitimacy of its cosmovision.

---

3. Fernando Cervantes, *The Devil in the New World* (New Haven: Yale University Press, 1994).

Conversion to the way of Jesus is beautiful. It is not a call to self-destruction. Conversion takes place not against one's tradition but within it. Conversion certainly means a dying to sin, but it does not mean a total destruction of one's way of life for the sake of another equally sinful cultural way of life. In fact, the worst sin of all is the failure to recognize our own inner and outer dignity, beauty, and infinite worth. This is the great sin of all those — many among the oppressed minorities — who in their innermost being accept any image of their inferiority and worthlessness. Conversion is about recognizing the fact that regardless of what the world says about us, we are neither inferior nor superior to anyone else — we are all different, but we are all equally children of God. Conversion is about recognizing the God-created goodness that lies within each of us and each and every people of the globe. Authentic conversion does not condemn anyone to servitude or make anyone ashamed of the ways of his or her ancestors. As Orlando Espín notes:

> To trample on the culture of a human group, therefore, cannot be justified in the name of the Christian God, because it would imply a denial of the incarnation of grace.... To trample on Hispanic culture while pretending to evangelize it is to impede the very experience of the God that saves.[4]

Unfortunately, evangelization during the second millennium of the Christian movement has ignored the way of the incarnation and substituted for it the way of cultural infusion and domination. In the evangelization of the Americas, the Europeans, using their own culturally determined image of "a good, mature, and civilized human being," judged the natives to be mere children, creators of tales, liars, and totally untrustworthy.[5] As such, they were judged incapable of preaching the gospel, understanding the dogmas of the faith properly, or being called to convent life or to sacred or-

---

4. Orlando Espín, "Grace and Humanness," in *We Are a People,* ed. Roberto Goizueta (Philadelphia: Fortress Press, 1992), 147.

5. Ana María Pineda, "Evangelization of the 'New World': A New World Perspective," *Missiology* 20, no. 2 (1992): 158.

ders.[6] They could be peripheral members of the church but could never participate fully in the life of the church. The Latin American church has not yet seen the full disastrous consequences of this crucial, long-standing error. A huge ecclesial superstructure has been built and maintained, but no real and lasting foundation has been provided for it to stand the test of ages. If no native clergy is allowed to emerge, the church will never take deep root in the local culture of the people.

The great conquistador himself, Cortés, sincerely desired to convert the Indians so that they might be saved, as is evident from the eyewitness accounts of his march into Mexico. But that "salvation" entailed the physical destruction of everything that had been sacred to the Indian world. Missioner and conquistador alike were participants in the common enterprise of tearing down ancient civilizations for the sake of building a new civilization according to European models. Whether for gold or for God, this meant downgrading the humanity of the Indians in favor of upgrading the humanity of the Europeans, and the ultimate justification of this was the God of the invaders. Since the ultimate legitimization of all this was God, it was only logical that the ultimate authority of the new civilization would be God's official spokesperson: the bishop.

In the Guadalupe event, all persons are called to conversion from that which imprisons them and robs them of the fullness of life; from that which enslaves them and keeps them from being free children of God; from that which blinds them and keeps them from appreciating themselves and others as God appreciates each one. Conversion is the great equalizer, for it calls everyone to the life and freedom of the children of God. Some will come down while others will be lifted up; some will discover doubts while others will arrive at new assurance; some will come to recognize their sinfulness while others will recognize their saintliness. Conversion brings about a blossoming of everything that is authentically human — the image and likeness of God.

---

6. Robert Ricard, *The Spiritual Conquest of Mexico: The Evangelizing Methods of the Mendicant Orders in New Spain, 1523–1572,* trans. Lesley Byrd Simpson (Berkeley: University of California Press, 1966), 226.

Of Persons: The New Juan Diego

Juan Diego is converted from the pain of social nonbeing
to becoming a full, confident, and joyful human person. He is
transformed from his debasement and shame to a new, confident
self-image. His psychological castration is healed. He is now a full
man; he is now an integral human being! He is free, trusted, and
self-assured. He goes forth full of the inner joy of being at ease with
himself. On his way to the bishop's palace with the requested sign,
Juan Diego is a totally different person than the broken-down man
we had met earlier:

> *He was in a hurry and very happy; his heart felt very sure and*
> *secure.... He was enjoying the scent of the beautiful flowers.*
> (v. 89)

In his dealings with the church officials, Juan is timid and subservient. After his encounters with them, he returns crushed,
humiliated, and disfigured. They had convinced him that he was
not trustworthy, that his word did not count, that he really did not
know what life was about. The church workers had convinced him
he was nothing but useless rubbish:

> *"With great difficulty I entered the place of the lord of the*
> *priests.... He received me well and listened carefully. But by*
> *the way he answered me, as if his heart had not accepted it, [I*
> *know] he did not believe it.... I saw perfectly, in the way he*
> *answered me, that he thinks that possibly I am just making*
> *it up that you want a temple to be built on this site.... I am*
> *one of those campesinos, a piece of rope, a small ladder, the*
> *excrement of people; I am a leaf; they order me around, lead*
> *me by force."* (vv. 36–40)

For Juan Diego, the church of the foreign and dominant culture, of
the conquistadors, is not a place of grace and salvation. He had
been accepted by the church and tolerated, but he was not appreciated or respected. His recently imposed inferiority had been
reinforced by the ministers of the God of the new religion — he

was not credible. The church preached love and compassion, but it practiced contempt and disregard for the cultural/racial "otherness" of the Indians. The missioners were the great protectors of the Indians and of the poor, but they could not tolerate the radical otherness of the new racial-cultural identity they were encountering. They would give their lives in the defense of the abused Indians, but they could not stomach the Indians as Indians, and they could certainly not conceive of the Indians (and later on Africans) as religious or priests. As one very committed Euro-American missioner recently told me: "We are happy to go work among them, but God forbid that we should have to live with them in the same house."

As I have stressed numerous times above, the final proof of the missioner's ultimate rejection of the Indian nations was their refusal to call them to holy orders or to allow them into religious life. It is hard to believe that this has gone on for five hundred years and in many ways continues today. No wonder the power of Nuestra Señora continues to increase.[7] I sometimes wonder if the rise of fundamentalism and especially Pentecostalism, which quickly calls native peoples to full ministry, is not God's punishment of the Catholic Church for refusing to call the non-European peoples to the full ordained ministry of the church.

It is interesting that the very same accusations of demon-worship, idolatry, and false worship and the same arguments against the fallacies of the native religious ways that the first missioners used are being used today by fundamentalist and Pentecostal ministers in relation to Latin American Catholicism. Are today's fundamentalist preachers the spiritual descendants of the early missioners? In many ways, they seem to be, though with one crucial difference: they quickly trust and call the native people to be the preachers of the word, something Catholics are still very hesitant to do.

As Juan Diego ascends Mount Tepeyac, as the Indians' ancient priests had ascended to the top of their pyramid-temples, he is

---

7. For a good documentary account of this, see Jeanette Rodríguez, *Our Lady of Guadalupe: Faith and Empowerment among Mexican-American Women* (Austin: University of Texas Press, 1993).

called by name by the Lady from Heaven. He goes to the source of life to be re-created a new person. In his rehabilitation, he will be her priest; he will be her trusted and necessary messenger; that is, he will be the one who will proclaim the word of the Mother of God, and in his very newness of life he will give witness to that word's re-creating power. In speaking to him, the Lady often refers to him as *"my most abandoned son, dignified Juan"* (v. 20). The contrast is between what the world abandons as worthless or trash and the secret known and revealed by the Lady: he is most dignified. He is truly a person of the wisdom not only of his own people but of the Mother of God.

The Lady could have chosen other messengers, but she finds it *"in every way precise"* that the most abandoned, most dignified Juan be her trusted messenger to the bishop, the supreme commander of the new, conquering group. She inserts Juan Diego into the biblical tradition of God's choice of the world's unnoticed, unwanted, and rejected. She does not call upon one of the ordained clergymen but on a simple, faithful man who is seeking God. The Spanish power will no longer be any match for Juan. In his newfound self-hood and divine commission, he will fear no one and confront anyone with the message of the Mother of God.

Juan Diego is converted from seeing himself and thinking of himself as the oppressors saw him to appreciating himself as God knows and appreciates him. This is the new life-giving power of God erupting in the poor who through God's call begin to believe in themselves. Regardless of what the world might say about them, they are God's dignified and trusted messengers. God calls them to collaborate in the building of a new temple, of a new way of life centered on love and compassion. This is the beginning of the new creation of the Americas.

Of Peoples

Salvation is not just about the hereafter. It begins in the here and now — for instance, with the healing of Juan Bernardino. The healing of Juan Bernardino is the first in an endless list of miracles brought about by Our Lady of Guadalupe. The missioners had been speaking about eternal salvation: suffer now and get your reward later in the afterlife. Our Lady never speaks about the soul or about eternal salvation or damnation. She is interested in the immediate salvation of her people. Her presence is to have immediate results, and the people are to experience her saving powers in their very flesh:

> *On the next day, Monday, when Juan Diego was supposed to take something to be the sign by which he was to be believed, he did not return, because when he arrived home, one of his uncles, named Juan Bernardino, had caught the smallpox and was in his last moments.*
>
> *First he went to call a doctor, who helped him, but he could do no more because he [Juan Bernardino] was already gravely ill. Through the night, his uncle begged him that while it was still dark, he should go to Tlatelolco to call a priest to come and hear his confession and prepare him well because he felt deeply in his heart that this was the time and place of his death, that he would not be healed.* (vv. 60–62)

The text is quite clear. Juan Bernardino is dying from the plague caused by the Europeans, and there is no hope of a cure. Everything is finished, so he must accept the situation and prepare himself for death. It appears there is nothing else to do, that no other course of action is possible. It is the darkness of the final moments of life, when everything comes to an end in the darkness of death. Without question or hesitation, Juan Diego decides that he must first take care of his dying uncle and then attend to the things of God. He sets out in haste to find the priest to confess his dying uncle. But on the way, even though he has made an effort to avoid the Lady so as not to be detained, she finds him, and after he has apologetically explained his actions to her, she assures him of his uncle's healing.

> *After hearing Juan Diego's discourse, the most pious Virgin answered: "Listen and hear well in your heart, my most*

*abandoned son: that which scares you and troubles you is
nothing; do not let your countenance and heart be troubled;
do not fear that sickness or any other sickness or anxiety. Am
I not here, your mother? Are you not under my shadow and
my protection? Am I not your source of life? Are you not in
the hollow of my mantle where I cross my arms? Who else
do you need? Let nothing trouble you or cause you sorrow.
Do not worry because of your uncle's sickness. He will not
die of his present sickness. Be assured in your heart that he is
already healed." (And as he learned later on, at that precise
moment, his uncle was healed.)* (vv. 75–77)

Five times the Lady tells him not to worry about Juan Bernardino's
sickness or any other illness; and five times she assures him that
she, his mother, is there to hold him in her bosom. Nothing in
heaven or earth is to trouble him. As noted earlier, in Nahuatl
thought, the number five indicates the meeting point of the ways
of God and the ways of human beings; it signifies the place and the
moment where the greatest contradictions are resolved through the
work of divine mercy in cooperation with the human endeavor.[8] It
is a moment of cosmic and historic creation. With the cooperation
of the Indian, God will bring about complete rehabilitation, and
there is nothing to worry about, no burden so heavy that it will
not be overcome. Juan Diego is the firstborn, and the rehabilitated
Juan Bernardino is the sign and guarantee that all will receive this
new life. The dying victims have been transformed into struggling
survivors. Survival is their victory over death. Their very survival
in spite of the worst odds is a sign of God's power unto life even
against the threats of death. In the healing of Juan Bernardino, the
entire people are rehabilitated and guaranteed survival against any
and all odds.

Juan Bernardino is converted from a dying sickness to life. For
the native peoples, this was an assurance of the continuation of the
way of life of their ancestors. For the native world the continu-

---

8. Clodomiro L. Siller Acuña, *Para comprender el mensaje de María de Guada-lupe* (Buenos Aires: Editorial Guadalupe, 1989), 62, 83.

ity of life was assured through the maternal uncle. The restoration
to health of the dying uncle is the sign that the way of life that
the Spaniards were trying to destroy and uproot would not die. It
would survive in new and unsuspected ways. In the rehabilitation
of the dying uncle, the way of life of the native nations is recognized, rehabilitated, and ennobled. The natives do not have to
become like the Spaniards to become Christians. They can receive
the saving graces of God as they are and thus bring forth a new
expression of Christianity that would enrich the entire fellowship
of Christians, making it ever more universal.

It was a divine affirmation of the way of life of their ancestors,
of their traditions and customs, of their music and dances, of their
religious expressions and beliefs. Conversion to the religion of the
Lady would definitely be transformative but not destructive of their
ways. This was authentic evangelization, for Jesus had come not to
destroy but to bring to perfection; not to divide but to welcome all
into the kingdom; to unite not through the uniformity of the world
but through the diversity of the Spirit.

The restoration to life of the dying uncle on December 12 was
nothing less than a historical resurrection of the dying peoples of
the Americas who now came to life as the new Christian people of
the Americas. Through Our Lady, a collective resurrection of the
people would take place. The healing of Juan Bernardino constituted the assurance of survival through the new way of life of the
Mother of Tepeyac. The people who had wanted only to die now
began to want to live. This was the source of their dancing, feast-
ing, and joy. They were crucified but not destroyed, crushed but
not held down, for in her they were (and are) alive, risen, and at the
beginning of a new life. Thus, liturgically, for us in the Americas,
December 12 is as important a feast as December 25 and Easter
Sunday are for the Christians of the Old World.

In the rehabilitation of Juan Bernardino, a totally new chapter in evangelization begins that will not be written about until
our own times: evangelization by way of the incarnation. In
the healing of Juan Bernardino, the conversion unto life of the
people truly begins. In him begins the mestizo Christianity of the
Americas.

Of Religions: Conversion of the Church

When the lord bishop saw her, he and all who accompa-
nied him fell to their knees and were greatly astonished. They
stood up to see her; they became saddened; their hearts and
their minds became very heavy.
  The lord bishop, with tears and sadness, prayed to her and
begged her to forgive him for not having believed her will, her
heart, and her word. (vv. 108–9)

This is a simple statement of the sorrow that leads through repentance and conversion to the blossoming of new life. The Lady had
given not only the requested sign but much more. She gave her
very self imprinted on the *tilma* of Juan Diego. The bishop and
his household saw, repented, and believed. This is the beginning of
the new partnership between the Indians as Indians and the Euro-
Christian church. Now a new church could truly be born, a new
common home for all the inhabitants of these lands.

Bishop Juan de Zumárraga and his household were converted
from confident control of the missionary process to humble sub-
mission. It was not easy for the bishop. After all, he had been
ordained, anointed, and canonically appointed to be the chief evangelizer and defender of the divine truth entrusted by Christ to the
church. As a white Westerner of his time, he had no doubts about
the universal superiority of the European way of life, in spite of
its corrupt ways, and canonically he had to defend the orthodoxy
of the church. As a Spanish Catholic, he had no doubts about the
church's absolute and exclusive claim to truth. One either was in
the church or was an infidel or heathen unworthy of life. His love
for the Indians, coupled with his apostolic zeal, which included his
ferocious desire to destroy and uproot all traces of native idolatry, made him a great religious warrior. His mission was clear and
urgent: to eradicate paganism and install the one true church. He
had, we can be sure, no identity crisis or doubts about his mission.
Such persons are the toughest to convert.

Here we get to the ultimate point of the narrative: the conversion of the bishop and his household — theologians, catechists,

liturgists, canonists, and others. The entire narrative calls them to convert from confident religious ethnocentrism to a position of doubt, curiosity, investigation, and finally conversion. Something new was happening. They were invited into it, but it was not within their control. They had been inviting (threatening?) the Indians to come to their churches, but now the Indians were requesting a temple into which the Spaniards would be invited on an equal footing with all the inhabitants of these lands. This was not an uprising. It did not just involve new arguments offered by the learned *tlamatini* (wise men/theologians) of the Nahuatl[9] against the presentations of the missioners. Rather it was an invitation — a demand — for a common enterprise.

The conversion of the bishop and his household to this new enterprise was, however, hard fought. With the fullest respect for the office of the bishop, Juan Diego had earlier persisted in the Lady's request and, after having been turned aside once, had returned a second time with exactly the same story and demand:

> *But the lord bishop asked him many questions; he interrogated him as to where he saw her and all about her so as to satisfy his heart. And he told the lord bishop everything.*
>
> *But even though he told him everything,... he still did not believe him.* (vv. 52–53)

The entire complex of events at Tepeyac was as mysterious as it was ultimately real. The bishop was disconcerted and his household was disturbed, as theologians, liturgists, and catechists usually are with the ways of God's poor. To this day, liturgists do not want to accept the feast of Our Lady of Guadalupe as the major feast of Advent. For them, it seems that God made a mistake in placing the feast of Guadalupe during Advent.

So Juan Diego faced not only befuddlement but downright resistance. In light of this the persistence of this poor Indian becomes all the more intriguing. He was not arguing doctrinally or dogmatically; he was not threatening to impose the Lady's will through physical force; he was not appealing to magical powers of any

---

9. Siller Acuña, *Para comprender el mensaje*, 62–67.

kind. His power was only his simplicity, patience, persistence, and meekness. Those means, however, took on a spiritual energy that began to pierce through to the mind and heart of the bishop with the force of a laser beam. Finally, the bishop could content himself no more. He asked for a sign:

> He [the bishop] told him that he could not proceed on her wishes just on the basis of his word and message. A sign from her would be necessary for the bishop to believe that he [Juan Diego] was indeed sent by the Lady from Heaven. When Juan Diego heard this, he told the bishop: "My patron and my lord, what is the sign that you want? [When I know, I can] go and ask the Lady from Heaven, she who sent me here."
> (vv. 54–55)

Juan Diego did not hesitate. After all, he had never doubted the Lady. No sign had been necessary for him to believe. But the bishop and the church needed one, and Juan Diego had no doubt the Lady would oblige. The beginning of this great miracle was that the bishop finally came to listen to the voice and call of the poor, ridiculed, crushed, and often ignored. The Mother of God gave the sign so that the bishop would begin to believe the poor, those who have no academic titles or canonical mandates. This points to the absurdity and foolishness of the God of the Bible: those who the world is convinced have nothing of value to offer have the greatest human and divine treasures to offer all of humanity. The church has been very slow in listening to the poor, and the academicians have been even slower. Only in recent times have the official ministers of the church moved from a mere tolerance of the Guadalupe event, from a domestication and self-serving manipulation of its inner force, to a real acknowledgment of its pastoral depth, its ability to be truly life-giving and liberating for the people.[10]

---

10. Richard Nebel, *Santa María Tonantzin: Virgen de Guadalupe* (Mexico City: Fondo de Cultura Económica, 1995), 324ff.; and Hugo D. Rivera Herrera, *Presencia de Santa María de Guadalupe en el pueblo mexicano* (Mexico City: Editorial Progreso, 1994).

At Tepeyac, the church is called to a deep metanoia from an overconfidence in its evangelizing programs and methods, based on the ways of the dominant and the powerful of this world, to a sincere surrender to the ways of God, who continues to come through the poor and the simple, those who are hurting and crying, the crucified and the dying. Today the entire church of the Western world is urgently being called to this profound metanoia.

It is important that we learn from the greatness of the first bishop of the Americas, who was able to break free from the imprisonment of his cultural-historical view of being church and to go out to build a new church with the disinherited of this world. Many in the church have fought against this conversion vehemently. The church has been very slow in converting, but it is on the way. Fundamentalists and Pentecostals are even slower in grasping the full meaning of Guadalupe, but Our Lady's tenderness and love will bring them about. The Latin American bishops' conferences at Medellín, Puebla, and Santo Domingo, the U.S. bishops' letters on social, cultural, and racial justice, and recent papal teachings on all questions of justice have certainly been good signs. The pope's creation of a Guadalupe chapel right next to the tomb of St. Peter in Rome is indicative of his own intuition of the uniqueness of Guadalupe in the universal evangelizing mission of the church.

The greatest challenge of Guadalupe continues to be the conversion of those who believe themselves to be Christian while actually being quite non-Christian. As I said earlier, it is much easier to convert a non-believer than those who are convinced they are already Christians. In Senegal in 1992, John Paul II spoke with great emotion and sorrow when he begged forgiveness for the atrocities of the "so-called Christians" of Europe who had enslaved millions of human beings for their own gain, honor, and glory. Their horror of the idols of the native religions kept them from seeing their own idols of profit and gold, and later on the religious absolutism of great monasteries allowed the missioners to sacrifice the Indians for the sake of the honor and glory of the religious orders. Worldly power made following Jesus impossible for those obsessed with gold and religious absolutism.

Only through conversion, the daily ecclesial conversion that
Paul VI speaks about in *Evangelii Nuntiandi,* can the church remain an authentic agent of a gospel way of life for the Americas.
In order to teach, the church must first listen compassionately to
the cries and laments of the people; it must enter into loving and
respectful dialogue with the peoples, their customs, and their religious traditions.[11] The early missioners in the Americas spoke
to the natives, and the natives were to listen; Our Lady comes
to listen — she wants a temple where she and the entire church
can listen to the voice of the hurting and neglected people. Jesus
listened for thirty years before he started teaching, and the missionary church must always be a listening church before it can be
a teaching church, teaching right out of the culture, tradition, and
experiences of the people. Jesus truly became one of his people in
every way before he started to invite them into a new life. This
is the way of the incarnation, and there can be no other way for
the church if it wants to be an authentic witness of the gospel (see
Vatican II, *Ad Gentes*). This was precisely the type of evangelization that Bartolomé de las Casas, along with others, was trying to
carry out, but he was considered a madman by most of his con-
temporaries.[12] The gospel method of evangelizing has no room for
the zealous destruction of what the missioner cannot understand
or appreciate. It is through the cries of the poor and rejected that
God continues to call the church to conversion to the way of Jesus,
and it is through the conversion of everyone that a new humanity
begins to blossom from within the earth of the Americas.[13]

*They took Juan Bernardino to the bishop so that he might
speak and witness before him. And, together with his nephew
Juan Diego, he was hosted by the bishop in his home for sev-*

---

11. This was the missionary model of the early church, which evangelized without the support of any worldly power. It is the missionary model proposed by the
missionary decree of Vatican Council II, *Ad Gentes*.

12. Miguel León-Portilla, *Endangered Cultures* (Dallas: Southern Methodist
University Press, 1990).

13. Opening address of Pope John Paul II at the Latin American bishops'
conference at Puebla, Mexico, in 1979.

eral days, until the hermitage of the Queen and Lady from Heaven was built at Tepeyac, where Juan Diego had seen her.

And the lord bishop transferred to the major church the precious image of the Queen and Lady from Heaven; he took her from the oratory of his palace so that all might see and venerate her precious image.

The entire city was deeply moved; they came to see and admire her precious image as something divine; they came to pray to her. They admired very much how she had appeared as a divine marvel, because absolutely no one on earth had painted her precious image. (vv. 120–24)

– 5 –

Mestizo Christianity

The new creation of the Americas begins with the Guadalupe conversion of everyone in these lands. The Guadalupe creation stories are as simple, as filled with image-poetry, and as beautiful as the stories found in Genesis 1 and 2. In the "little stories" of Juan Diego as known and transmitted by the ordinary people one can find the "big story"[1] of the struggles for identity, recognition, belonging, and dignity of the new and emerging humanity of the Americas, of the truly new creation taking place within the American continent.

Original Christianity

In every movement of peoples, whether it be migration, exile, or conquest, there is a mutual and yet unbalanced cultural influence — the dominant group has the greater impact because they control the image of the good, the true, and the beautiful human being and have the means to enforce and impose their cosmovision on everyone else. The early Christian movement went against this current and, working from the perspective of the new cosmovision of the converted poor and disenfranchised who now saw them-

---

1. For a very creative and critical discussion of how universal truth can be found in the little stories of the people, see Alejandro García-Rivera, *St. Martin de Porres: The "Little Stories" and the Semiotics of Culture* (Maryknoll, N.Y.: Orbis Books, 1995).

selves and everyone else in a radically new way, started to change all the people it encountered, regardless of the perceived superiority of these peoples.

Through the force of their conversion to the way of Jesus, the poor, the slaves, and the servants (i.e., the people who were considered by the dominant as ignorant, inferior, rubbish, and without "culture") were no longer ashamed of who they were, nor did they feel inferior because of their socioeconomic, racial, or cultural status. They gained a new pride and a new confidence in their new identity and status as children of God that enabled them to enter into dialogue with the great, powerful cultures of the world on an equal status — neither fearing them nor wanting to imitate them. The poor and the nameless who had found a new wealth and identity now encountered the wealthy and the powerful, who were actually poor in the riches that really matter.

In the new universal fellowship from below, based on the "little stories" of Jesus of Nazareth, a new identity and status emerged that would transcend the previous identity struggles and dehumanizing divisions between men and women; Greeks, Jews, and Romans; masters and slaves; intellectual elites and the ignorant rabble; saints and sinners; citizens and foreigners; legals and illegals — for beyond all those worldly classifications, they were all first and foremost creatures of the one Creator and children of the same Parents. No one had to renounce or cease being who they were sexually, ethnically, racially, or otherwise, but they could be who they were in a radically new way — all equally dignified as children of the one God. A new fellowship could now be formed wherein all would truly be esteemed and respected brothers and sisters in the one family, all welcomed members of the one household, all sharing a common body and blood that were far greater and more noble than the flesh and blood of any earthly royalty. This was the beginning of the new culture brought about through the power of the Spirit.

It was a new paradigm for universalizing humanity not by making it all the same — eliminating differences and making it all uniform — but by relativizing all human differences in terms of the one absolute that is truly absolute: the unlimited love of God, Fa-

ther and Mother of all, experienced in the kingdom of God.[2] The
enthusiasm, conviction, and joy of the poor and marginated who
had been reborn into the wealth of love, compassion, and fellowship offered new hope for a peace, happiness, and tranquillity like
the world had never known. This was the contagious force that
carried Christianity to new cultures and peoples with greater speed
and energy than any of the conquering armies had ever achieved.[3]

Through these encounters originating from the bottom of society (see 1 Corinthians 1), the intellectual Hellenistic culture was
Christianized while Christianity was Hellenized; the powerful Roman culture was Christianized while Christianity was Romanized;
and the barbarian European tribes were Christianized while Christianity was Europeanized. This was the way of the incarnation, and
in every incarnation of this type there is a humanizing liberation of
the cultures involved, a humanizing of the ecclesial structures and
styles of worship, and a deepening in the understanding and appreciation of the gospel. A corollary of this, however, is that as
the gospel became incorporated into the dominant and victorious
cultures, it equally took on the ways and imagery of the reigning
civilizations.

This tradition of the ongoing incarnation of the gospel, which
had been dormant since the end of the first millennium, began anew in the Christianization of conquered and colonized
America. As this process has progressed, Christianity has been
incarnated not according to the conquering, colonizing, and dominating model of the European Christians (Protestant or Catholic)
but through the evangelizing witness of the converted poor and
marginated Indians, African-Americans, mestizos, and mulattos in
whom and through whom the original gospel witness is best seen,
heard, and experienced. It is through the Christianity of these
groups that America is still being Christianized and Christianity
is being genuinely Americanized. The European missioners planted

---

2. The kingdom (reign) of God is that space in one's heart and on earth where
the ultimate criterion for action and priorities is God's love that allows us to love
each other as God loves each one of us.

3. Pope Paul VI refers to this when at the beginning of *Evangelii Nuntiandi*
poses the question of "what has happened to the hidden energy of the Good
News?" (no. 4).

the seeds into the spiritual soil of these lands, and a truly new Christianity of the Americas took root and bloomed.

The Americas: A Crucible of Peoples

The Americas are known worldwide as the "New World," but they would be better named "the new race," for they are truly a crucible for the making of all the nations and races of the world. The Americas have given the poor, the broken, the enslaved, the disenfranchised, and the nameless from other continents — different stocks and traditions — the opportunity to unite. Peoples of all races, ethnic backgrounds, and religions come to the Americas seeking to be re-created into a new life of freedom, happiness, and opportunity, and in so doing, they contribute to the creation of a new America, or better yet, a new humanity of the Americas.

But the challenge of a truly new humanity of America can never be resolved without special attention to the natives who were conquered, colonized, exploited, to a large degree exterminated (biologically and/or culturally), and made to live as foreigners in their own lands and at the margins of the great American dream. Neither can we ignore the millions of Africans who were brought to the Americas by force and condemned to a life of slavery and misery. It is true that blacks have been emancipated, but they have not yet been recognized as fully human and given equal opportunity in the structures of society. Further, the mestizos and mulattos not only have suffered the fate of the natives and the Africans but have also suffered the fate of not being recognized as fully human by anyone. Nowhere in the Americas could they feel at home and experience a sense of belonging. Yet it is within this rapidly expanding mestizo/mulatto identity that the new America is emerging.[4]

Whereas racial mixture was rapid and wholesale in much of Latin America, ethnic mixing, even among European immigrants,

---

4. For a further discussion on this topic, see my own works *Galilean Journey: The Mexican-American Promise* (Maryknoll, N.Y.: Orbis Books, 1983), and *The Future Is Mestizo: Life Where Cultures Meet* (New York: Crossroad, 1988).

has been slow in the United States, Argentina, and Chile as the peoples from the Old World have struggled to maintain a type of ethnic purity by intermarrying among themselves. Racial mixture became a cornerstone of Latin America, and, even though it was prohibited by law in the United States, it still took place there. Whether one likes this mixture or not, it is a fact of life. No one group can remain so isolated and pure that it will not be affected in some way by the others. There is no doubt that the dominant northern European and Iberian cultures have had a much greater impact on everyone, yet they too are affected by the others.[5]

The tragedy of the Americas has not been racial mixture (in fact that has been the source of the Americas' deepest and most creative newness) but the shame inflicted upon the children of this mixture and their "inferior" parent, most usually the mother.[6] Since the beginning of the European invasion of the Americas, the white European — the northern European Protestant in North America and the Iberian Catholic in Latin America — has been installed as the norm of trueness, goodness, and beauty. Segregation was imposed by the white Europeans with a biological rationale. For many white people, their own interiorized self-image of superiority remains unquestioned even today. For Juan Ginés de Sepúlveda — a great defender of the colonial mission — conquest and evangelization were a great service to humanity since the Spanish were "prudent, powerful, and perfect people" while the Indians were "barbarian, uncultured, and inhuman."[7] Europeans viewed their civilization and their version of Christianity as superior to all others and as divinely chosen for the governing of the world. The result of this has

---

5. It is well documented that the children of Spaniards who grew up in Mexico became much different from the Peninsular-born Spaniards due to the influence of the Indian cultures. The Indian cultures had a great influence in bringing about a sense of gentleness, respect for the elders, politeness in language, and so on. This is clearly evidenced today in the great difference between the Spanish of Spain and the "Spanish" of Latin America, especially in the countries where the greatest *mestizaje* took place, such as Mexico, the Central American nations, Colombia, Ecuador, Peru, and Bolivia.

6. For an in-depth discussion of this sense of shame, see Darcy Ribiero, "The Latin American People," in *1492–1992: The Voice of the Victims,* ed. Leonardo Boff and Virgil Elizondo (London: SCM Press, 1990).

7. Casiano Floristán, "Evangelization of the 'New World': An Old World Perspective," *Missiology* 20, no. 2 (1992): 143.

been to delegate all others, especially people who were not European, to a status of inferiority, silence, and servitude that justified exploitation of all types.

But even deeper than the external exploitation was the interior pain and spiritual destructiveness that it caused, as it led many of the oppressed to become ashamed of their very being — their race, their language, their traditions, and their whole way of being. Many, unfortunately often with the help of Christian missioners who were trying to "save them," even came to see their inferiority as a punishment from God for the ways of their ancestors.

The children of the sexual union of oppressed and oppressor were especially affected by this self-denigration. Since most of the cases of race mixture were the results of European fathers mating with Indian or African women, and since in most of these cases the fathers abandoned both mother and child, the children of these unions lived with a profound sense of nothingness and rejection. They longed to be accepted within the household of the father whom they had never known, knowing fully well that there they would never be accepted, respected, trusted, or valued. Yet they were not even "Indian" or "African" any more. No matter how much they might have wanted to be either white or nonwhite, they were constantly distanced from both. They were neither purely the oppressed nor the oppressor, neither a native nor a foreigner — for they were actually both and neither at the same time. This is the painful and devastating reality of the identity of cultural/racial nonbeing and nonbelonging.

Their identity was precisely in their nonidentity: there was no place where they truly belonged, felt at home. Many tried to emulate the European model of being human, but for that they were ridiculed, maligned, and rejected. In trying to prove themselves to be members of the dominant society, they frequently became worse with their own and with the people of their mother culture than the conquistadors themselves. The result was that they ended up being despised by both. This denial and splitting of identities only deepened the division and hatred between the diverse peoples. The conquest had given rise to a biological and cultural *mestizaje* with all its painful consequences of trying to live with

two or more distinct souls: one Western, the other native; one powerful, the other crushed; one oppressor, the other oppressed; one white, the other brown; one Christian, the other rooted in native religions. As a result of this, the racially mixed people had no proper soul, no proper body, no proper space where they could truly be at home.

Anthropological Reversal

The inner re-creating power of Guadalupe, its anthropological reversal of the dynamics of the conquest, lies in the core of the "little story": the Indian Mother sends the Christian-Indian child to call the Christian father to become a home-builder.[8] Mother, child, and father interrelate in a new way and together become the image and likeness of God. The divine image of God as loving relationships can finally be seen and experienced in the Americas and thus become the basis of the new humanity. The integrity of the Mother, the rebirth of the conquered Indian, and the repentance of the conquering bishop give rise to the new mestizo soul of the new humanity of the Americas. This will be the basis of mestizo spirituality: openness to everyone without exception.

The Indian Mother demanding that the Spanish father build a home for her children was unheard-of in New Spain. It is a declaration that the women will no longer remain silent, passive, and subject to abuse. The introduction of the new paradigm of partnership is the beginning of the end of the patriarchal domination rooted in hierarchical structures imported and imposed by Europe. Through the medium of the Indian Mother and Juan Diego, the Spanish bishop undergoes a radical change. He will remain an essential component of the partnership but in a radically new way.

---

8. This could well provide an original American imagery as an alternative to the Old World's imagery of the Trinity. After Guadalupe, the triune God and the trinitarian life of Christians could be known and appreciated through the native imagery of the Americas, and this in turn would purify the Old World's imagery of the Trinity. The Old World seemed to believe that the only way to express the trinitarian relationship was through the patriarchal-hierarchical paradigm of Christianity; the natives cast this relationship in terms of egalitarian partnership.

His role as bishop is not eliminated; his Spanish identity is not crushed; he is simply related to the others in a new, egalitarian way. This is never easy for those in power to accept, but he too will now enter personally into the process of *mestizaje*. He will no longer be just a Spanish Christian.

The chief authority of the society now recognizes and affirms the dignity and legitimacy of what he and his people had considered inferior, superstitious, and diabolical. Those in power can now begin to see and appreciate the very sacredness of "the other" of their new world and in the same process be liberated from imprisonment by their own self-declared superiority, righteousness, and arrogance. The conversion of the bishop completes the good news — the *evangelium* — of the Guadalupe events. This represents the ongoing call to conversion, especially of those who use their positions to oppress, dominate, and exploit the weaker ones of society.

Given the cultural reality that was emerging following the conquest, the repentance of the bishop marks the beginning of the much needed repentance of fathers who abuse women and then abandon them and their children. It is also the beginning of the repentance of those — including most of the missioners — who with the best of intentions had imposed on the people and, rather than "saving" them, had contributed to their inner shame, alienation, and destruction.

For the church too this marks a radical rupture with the old evangelization based on the cultural-doctrinal principles and pedagogies of spiritual conquest. Guadalupe retrieved the original ways of evangelization through personal invitation, respect, patient dialogue between persons and cultures, and liberating and empowering conversion and communion in the new fellowship of the unconditional equality of God's children. Guadalupe initiated a new evangelization[9] that 450 years later would become part of

---

9. This type of evangelization was understood by great and visionary men like Bartolomé de las Casas, Vasco de Quiroga, and a few others. However, they were a voice crying in the desert — for the most part the church's policy was to discredit and destroy everything that appeared as pagan or diabolical. Even some of the finest missioners remained fearful of what they considered dangerous acculturation, and

the official evangelization process elaborated by Popes Paul VI and John Paul II.

You might say that this is the story of the prodigal father repenting and coming home to the merciful Mother so that they can live, work, and celebrate together with all their children. Here begins the inner transformation of the conquering culture: from domination to partnership; and of the conquered culture: from victimization to survival and creative development. This new partnership will evolve slowly over the centuries and is far from being complete. It will emerge as the basis of the national consciousness of a mestizo people, a consciousness that is inclusive of everyone and that will become the basis not only of independence but of reclaiming the original native name: México; that will become the basis of the liberating *pastoral Guadalupana* that is being initiated; and that will grow into recognition of Guadalupe as the Mother of the Americas.

The conversion process associated with the "spiritual conquest" demanded that the Indians give up the ultimate ground of their existence without ever being fully recognized as equal to the European Christians. Converted Indians would become cultural mestizos and would thus join the ranks of the mestizo homeless of the Americas. Juan Diego was biologically fully Indian, but culturally he was a fledgling mestizo, for he was on the way to church to learn about the new religion that the Spaniards had brought. He was in the process of being emptied of the wisdom, values, and traditions of his people so as to replace them with those of the religion of New Spain. From being a respected wise man of his people, he would become a silent learner. This would make him a despised foreigner among his own people and a mere "mission Indian" for the Spaniards. Never and nowhere would he ever again experience being a full and integral human being; never again would he have a true home. He would be a "coconut": brown on the outside, white on the inside.

---

they always maintained the final word on what could remain and what had to be eliminated in the Indians' culture and worship. For further information on this, see Miguel León-Portilla, *Endangered Cultures* (Dallas: Southern Methodist University Press, 1990), 87–122.

At this time there was a sharp division between the natives who accepted the religion of the invaders and the ones who held on to their ancestral religions, religion being the ultimate nonnegotiable division among peoples. By accepting the new religion, Juan Diego accepted being marginated from his own people while not being accepted as a full and mature human being by those of the new religion. I am sure some of his people looked upon him, as most mestizos have been looked upon by their mother cultures, as a traitor. After all, the most scandalous form of perversion for the Nahuatl world was the abandonment of the traditions and religion of the ancestors.[10] By going to instruction and accepting the culture and religion of the Spaniards, he was abandoning his own people and even his ancestors.

But Juan Diego will astonish and surprise everyone. The Indian Mother of God changed everything and made new ways possible for everyone. He will be a Christian but not a traitor. Now the spiritual *mestizaje* begins as all begin to share in a common mestizo soul. He will no longer be a person without a proper identity and a space of belonging. Without renouncing his incipient Christianity, he reclaims the faith of his ancestors and dares to go to the bishop to demand a new partnership, a common enterprise, in building a home for the Indian Mother of everyone. He does not just take sides with the new culture-religion but rather goes to its headquarters to demand a change, and, going further, he demands this change in the name of the one Mother of God: the God of the Spaniards and the God of his ancestors and their religious traditions. Juan Diego is the prototype of the converted Indian for whom conversion does not mean an abandonment of his cultural heritage.

Through this spiritual *mestizaje*, the conquered reclaim the legitimacy, veracity, beauty, and sacredness of the values and traditions of their people while through the same spiritual *mestizaje* the European invaders are graced with a new humility and openness so as to see and appreciate the gifts of God that they had ignored or disdained in peoples who were different from them. Both would begin

---

10. León-Portilla, *Endangered Cultures*, 68–73.

to experience a cure of their anthropological blindness and a liberation of their spirit that would enable them to cross the ultimate barriers of separation.

For the first time, an equal respect and valorization of both of the parent cultures were made possible. A true dialogue of persons and of cultures, which had proved to be totally impossible in the colloquiums of the Franciscan theologians with the Nahuatl theologians,[11] now began to take place through the mediation of a new partner (Tonantzin/Guadalupe), a mediation that enabled both to see and appreciate each other in new ways neither had previously suspected. This dialogue of two very different humanities through the medium of Tonantzin/Guadalupe not only liberated and ennobled the Spaniards and the Indians alike but equally opened the way for the ongoing inclusion of new partners beginning with their mestizo children. Yet this dialogue would not be easy or fast because of the multifaceted and more powerful force of the colonial structures. That dialogue would be, and continues to be, hindered and blocked in many ways by many diverse interests. But, at least, the doors had been opened and the process had been started for an eventual eschatological fulfillment.

With the emergence of the mestizo soul, Juan Diego goes with confidence to call the father to come build a home for the Mother and all their children. How could the father refuse such a beautiful and dignifying request? The child calls the father to recognize, legitimize, and honor the new family that he has started by building a home where the Mother can be honored and venerated and she in turn can show her love and compassion to the entire family. The new home to be built for the Virgin Mother by the father/bishop will be for all their children of the Americas — finally, a common home for all the inhabitants. This is the very opposite of what was happening and what unfortunately is still the scandalous reality of the Americas, with the churches often accepting these sinful situations in a silent and condoning way. At Tepeyac, the abused and abandoned woman becomes the cherished Mother while the abusive and runaway father becomes the respectful and loving

---

11. Léon Portilla, *Endangered Cultures*, 70–73.

home-builder, constructing a home wherein all the children without exception or condition can be equally proud of their racial, cultural, and religious ancestry. The conversion is from the shame and sorrow of abandoned orphanhood to the pride and joy of ancestral origins.

Juan Diego fulfills the necessary mediating role of the mestizo: he mediates the perspective of the people of the abused culture to the powerful, demanding that they change their entire way of acting, viewing, thinking about, and judging the humanity that they had abused. Juan Diego is the new mestizo who is no longer ashamed of the ways of his people and his ancestors, nor fearful of and subservient to the ways of the dominant. Rather, rooted in his abused cultural ancestors and in solidarity with them, he goes with pride, joy, and boldness to offer a new alternative to those in power. He acknowledges the presence and power of the new authorities (he really has no choice), but he no longer simply submits and gives in to them. He goes with persistence and confidence to offer something totally new from among his own people and his own traditions. Whereas the *mestizaje* of the conquest was destructive of everyone, the *mestizaje* of Guadalupe is reconstructive of everyone. Here begins the possibility of building a new cosmovision and reality that will include much of both cultures and races but, even more important, will surpass the limitations of the divisiveness of Western thought, the extremes of Iberian absolutism, and the cosmic fatalism of Nahuatl religion. This is the Tepeyac-temple that the Indian Mother desires and demands, a temple wherein the anthropology of identity based on divisive differences will be transformed into one of identity based on unifying interconnectedness.

Evangelical Christianity

At Tepeyac no one is to be rejected. Tepeyac becomes the most sacred space of the Americas precisely because of the unlimited diversity of peoples who experience a common home there. Precisely because everyone is welcomed there and experiences a sense of belonging, is listened to with compassion and senses the energy of true universal fellowship, the face of God is clearly seen while the heart of God is experienced intimately and tenderly. This is what makes Tepeyac so sacred — it is not a sacredness that scares, separates, and divides but the sacredness of the holiness of God that allures, brings together, and unites.

In the events of Tepeyac, the process of unjust and dehumanizing segregation by sex, race, class, and ethnicity is totally reversed not by providing a finished humanity but by initiating a new process by which a truly new humanity recognizing the legitimacy, beauty, and dignity of each and every human group might gradually develop and come to be. Within the new process, *mestizaje* will be transformed from a source of shame and dislocation to a source of belonging and pride in each of the ancestral lines; this *mestizaje* will be the basis of the structuring and building up of the new family home — the new temple — wherein the mestizo/mulatto children and their European, African, and native parents will be equally recognized, cherished, and welcomed. They who had no place of their own will provide the new place for themselves, their parents, and future generations of new and exciting mixtures. They who in the beginning of the Americas had no home — whether they were natives or invaders — will now provide the new home for everyone.

What most people who have not experienced the Guadalupe tradition cannot understand is that to be a Guadalupano/a (one in whose heart Our Lady of Guadalupe reigns) is to be an evangelical Christian. It is to say that the Word became flesh in Euro-Native America and began its unifying task — "that all may be one." In Our Lady of Guadalupe, Christ became American. Yet because the gospel through Guadalupe was such a powerful force in the creation and formulation of the national consciousness and identity of the people as expressed, understood, and celebrated through their art, music, poetry, religious expression, preaching, political discourse, and cultural-religious celebrations, its original meaning — that is, the original gospel of Jesus expressed in and through native Mexican terms — has become eclipsed. This has led some modern-day Christians — especially those whose Christianity is expressed through U.S. cultural terms — to see Guadalupe as pagan or as something opposed to the gospel. It is certainly true that just as the gospel was co-opted and domesticated by Constantine and subsequent "Christian" powers, so has Guadalupe been co-opted and domesticated by the powerful of Mexico, including the church. Yet neither the initial gospel nor the gospel expressed through Guadalupe has lost its original intent or force, a force that is being rediscovered as the poor, the marginated, and the rejected reclaim these foundational gospels as their chief weapons of liberation and as sources of lifestyles that are different from those engendered by ecclesial and social structures that have marginalized, oppressed, and dehumanized them.

As primitive evangelical Christianity was at the heart of a balance between unifying the tribes and nations of the Old World while still allowing for their diversity, so Guadalupe is the very center and starting point of the synthesis of peoples of the Americas that will become the deepest ingredient and chief characteristic of the new humanity of the New World. European Christianity in the Americas could not be the unifying force evangelical Christianity had been for Europe because over the course of time, it had been transformed into a conquering Christendom that justified the European expansion and enslavement of peoples. Guadalupe did what European Christianity could not do for itself: it transformed conquering Christianity into evangelical Christianity. Out of the ranks of the dying but reborn Christians would begin the new spiritual/ Christian *mestizaje*, the new and all inclusive soul of the Americas. It begins as the child that Our Lady carries within her womb, recognized by Juan Diego as Jesus Christ, becomes alive in us and equally becomes the new center of all life — of all the cosmos.

— 6 —

Reflections on
the Guadalupe Event

The building of the new temple wherein all the inhabitants of the Americas will truly feel at home will demand much more than merely constructing a beautiful and spacious basilica at Tepeyac. The more difficult edifice to construct is a new world vision with its own understanding of truth, beauty, and goodness that will overcome the multiple limitations, divisions, distortions, and oppositions by which men and women are made opponents, enemies, or slaves of one another. It will be a temple of humanity in which love and justice will go hand in hand with an integral world vision to sustain its development and expansion.

The Guadalupe vision is not something totally new, for it is simply the ideal of the kingdom of God as lived and proclaimed by Jesus. This is the lifestyle and ideal that he died for. Guadalupe is the good news of the Christian movement that is recorded in the Gospels and lived and celebrated by Christians, especially in the Eucharist. What is uniquely new in Guadalupe is that it advances our understanding of Christianity in some very refreshing and stimulating ways.

Through the Guadalupe event and story, those whom the builders of this world's empires had maligned and rejected, re-created the gospel at every level of human existence. The Guadalupe event was a divine intervention for the sake of the gospel at the most unique moment in the recorded history of the Americas — the beginning of the New World. The full meaning of this new vision has not been explored and developed, but I am convinced

115

that the seeds of a new and unique knowledge of the Americas lies within the events, narrative, and image of Our Lady of Guadalupe. What follows are ideas that I hope will provoke thought, discussion, and debate that will assist all of us in the creation and formulation of a new knowledge and vision of the Americas.

It Is about Truth Itself

Guadalupe is not an isolated, abstract, doctrinal truth; neither is it a legal or moralistic truth. According to the Guadalupan vision, truth exists in the relational, the interconnected, the beautiful, and the melodic; it cannot be reduced to a single, essential element, for it is only in its totality, in its wholeness, that this truth can be perceived and appreciated. Ultimate truth cannot be corralled by definition; it can only be approximated through *flor y canto*. Thus what might appear as merely accidental to Western thought is of the very essence of reality in Guadalupe.

Guadalupe is the truth about truth itself. It introduces us to a new epistemology, for it has to do with the notion of truth and knowledge. In it, Western thought is intermingled with Nahuatl thought to produce a new knowledge and new forms of expression of this knowledge. It intermingles Western historiography with its Nahuatl counterpart.[1] It is also a new metaphysics, for it deals with reality itself — with what is ultimately real.[2]

The Nahuatl philosophers were as fascinated with reality and truth as Aristotle, Plato, and the other great Greek philosophers.[3] The strength of Nahuatl metaphysics was its emphasis on the interconnectedness and interdependence of all creation; its limitation or weakness was the submersion of the individual in the collectivity, even allowing the individual to be sacrificed for the sake of the collectivity. The strength of Western metaphysics has been

1. Richard Nebel, *Santa María Tonantzin: Virgen de Guadalupe* (Mexico City: Fondo de Cultura Económica, 1995), 235.

2. Nebel, *Santa María Tonantzin*, 234–64, esp. 261–63.

3. Miguel León-Portilla, *Aztec Thought and Culture* (Norman: University of Oklahoma Press, 1963).

the isolation and exaltation of the individual; its weakness has been the sacrifice of the collectivity, other individuals, and even the world for the sake of the strongest individual. Both have strengths and disastrous weaknesses. Both need one another to become complete.

Guadalupe merges the two into a new metaphysics that recognizes the interconnectedness and interdependence of all creation[4] while equally recognizing the uniqueness and value of the individual within the cosmic.[5] Furthermore, while recognizing the influence of the cosmic forces, it equally recognizes the determining role of our personal interventions in the historical process, thus bringing together and enriching both the Nahuatl concept of cosmic determinism and the Western concept of historical absolutism. For the Nahuatls, history was cyclic and predetermined by cosmic powers; for the Westerners, it was linear, determined by human endeavor alone, and often seemed to be composed of discrete, unconnected events. For Guadalupe, history is continuity with the past recycled into the new being of the future that begins in the present moment: the past and the future are alive in us.[6]

In the epistemology of Guadalupe, truth cannot be obtained or arrived at through observation, rational analysis, and argumentation alone, but can only be fully grasped through the beauty of sight and sound followed by critical questioning and analysis. Dreams and visions are as much a part of the process of discovering and knowing as critical observation and analysis of reality. This was the process Juan Diego went through to arrive at the truth of Our Lady of Guadalupe. No one aspect defined or proved the truth and authenticity of Our Lady at Tepeyac or of the new Juan Diego. Truth emerges in the totality of the events. The ultimate

---

4. In the opening scenes (v. 18), all the land, plants, and rocks around Tepeyac take on a new appearance in relation to Our Lady, and from the narrative it is clear that we are at the crossroads of all creation — at the point through which everything is connected.

5. This is evident in the way in which Juan Diego is singled out and treated with great affection, dignity, and respect throughout the entire narrative.

6. Our Lady appears as the mother of the gods of the ancestors (v. 22); Juan Bernardino is healed to assure the continuity with the life of the ancestors and with the new generations. History is characterized not by discrete, unconnected events but by continuity and transformation.

truth of Guadalupe is connected to the healing of the sick and
to wholeness, a truth clarified by the words transmitted through
Juan Diego.

For the Nahuatls, divine truth existed in *flor y canto;* no one
expression of truth could communicate the whole truth, especially
about God. According to this view, ultimate truth can be grasped
and expressed only through the poetic and the artistic, through
the beautiful and the rhythmic, through individuality and diversity. And there is no better medium for this than that of *flor y
canto.* For the Westerners of that time, divine truth existed in the
doctrinal proposition, in the logic- and reason-bound spoken or
written word. This view was mistrustful of the image and of poetry. Creeds and dogmas were held to express the ultimate essence
and nature of truth and revelation. Thus the quest for definition and orthodoxy, for universal absolutes and abstract essences,
has dominated Western thought and prevented it from appreciating the positive role of differences. María Pilar Aquino notes that
Western thought is also marked by a logometric, impositional, conquering and colonial, one-sided, one-voiced, dualistic and abstract
character.[7]

In contrast, Guadalupe is an image-word that is experienced
through the beauty of *flor y canto* and then explained through the
spoken (later written) words of Juan Diego. This combination allows us to understand not only with our minds but even more so
with our hearts. It allows us to see what we understand and to
understand what we see. Thus it alone allows us the experience
of complete human understanding, understanding of the mind and
the heart. Truth will be known through the synthesis of image,
beauty, and words. The synthesis constitutes what Christians call
the "word of God." It is neither the sensual and gut knowledge
of *flor y canto* alone, nor intellectual knowledge alone, but knowledge of the whole person involving all the avenues of knowing: the
senses, the mind, and the heart.

---

7. María Pilar Aquino, *Our Cry for Life: A Feminist Theology from Latin
America* (Maryknoll, N.Y.: Orbis Books, 1993), 71–77.

It Is about Evangelization and Faith

The apparition of Our Lady of Guadalupe is the beginning of the new evangelization, the one that Paul VI spoke about in 1975 and John Paul II has been so urgently calling for as the millennium comes to an end. We might summarize the evangelizing method, expression, and fervor of the Guadalupe process by stating that it proceeded by way of beauty, initiated a gradual dialogue, was most respectful of the evangelized, and empowered them with new life. Because it invited the evangelized to an experience of the divine, into a mystical experience, it produced security, joy, and excitement. It did not just speak about God and the teachings of God; it invited the participant into intimate contact and friendship with God. This mystical experience of the presence of God is at the core of the new evangelization.

The method of Guadalupe is based on beauty, recognition and respect for "the other," and friendly dialogue. It is based on the power of attraction, not on threats of any kind. Juan Diego is attracted by the beautiful singing that he hears; he is fascinated by the gentleness and friendliness of the Lady, who by her appearance is evidently an important person; he is uplifted by her respectful and tender treatment of him; he is captivated by her looks. She is so important, yet she takes time to call him by name and to visit with him in a very friendly way. In her presence, he exhibits no inferiority or fears. Here there is no fear of hell — here, Juan Diego is experiencing heaven.

The old evangelization, as I have argued earlier, emphasized threats of hell and eternal damnation. Our Lady prefers to offer us a foretaste of heaven. This is the new method, which is actually the method of Jesus and which is supposed to be lived out in the Eucharist. The contrast between the old and the new is sharp. While the church was trying desperately to create vivid imagery of judgment, purgatory, and the eternal fires of hell, Our Lady of Guadalupe is giving Juan Diego a holistic experience of heaven. In her presence, he is transformed. And the final proof of the absolute truth of this experience is not the power and might of God proven in battle by the sword and the gun, but beautiful flowers with a heavenly aroma blooming on the desert hill top — and in the midst of winter! The ultimate sign of God's transforming power is the peaceful and miraculous flowering of new life in the midst of the deserts of human existence, not the destructive power of the growing military might of the modern world. The powerful had crucified Jesus, had executed him unjustly, but God raised him to life. The sign of this power of God has always been the beautiful flowers of Easter. Flowers, not weapons, are the signs of God's ultimate power over unjust executions and death.

Juan Diego was re-created through his contacts with the Lady. This was the basis of his enthusiasm, courage, and fervor. He goes hurriedly, with confidence and joy, to the bishop's house. When today's poor experience themselves as recognized, respected, and called by name by the living God, they take on God's cause for humanity with the same joy and conviction as Juan Diego. They are no longer victims and are now survivors. Their fiestas, dances, songs, poetry, and joy make God's presence come alive. This type of evangelizing ministry is working miracles in ordinary pastoral life in parishes throughout the Americas. I have experienced this joy and fervor among the early *cursillistas*, the charismatics, the people who participate in the *comunidades de base*, the people who participated in civil rights demonstrations, and the many new movements of the Spirit that are erupting spontaneously throughout the Christian world. This joy and fervor erupt when the faithful poor dare to defy the controlling and limiting rules and regulations of the dominant culture and its religious institutions and dare to converse directly with God in their own language and in the language of their ancestors. It is the joy of the poor who, far from giving in to despair, rejoice in recognizing the unique gifts God has bestowed upon them. A true Christian fiesta cannot be programmed or faked. It is experienced and lived.

In evangelization, the church should be less concerned with the fires of hell, which are all too evident all around us, and with rules and regulations, which are so overwhelming in our bureaucratic society. It should be concerned, rather, with creating foretastes of heaven here on earth. The people need to experience beautiful and transforming alternatives to the present-day world situation of violence, filth, misery, enslavement, and earthly damnation. The churches often speak about eternal damnation but ignore the earthly damnation that we have created for ourselves. People say "get tough on crime," but few seriously ask what is producing so much violence and crime. We have an overabundance of doctrinal truths, and we have had many arguments and fights over them, but we have been poor and lacking in beautiful truth, that is, the absolute and eternal truth that shines through and is experienced in beauty. We in the West have been strong on the rational and logical but very weak on and suspicious about the mystical and poetic. We are afraid of dreams and apparitions, even though the Bible is full of them, because they are beyond our control, and it seems that we cannot accept what we cannot control. The God of dreams, who is beyond our control, seems to be the opponent of the God of reason and creeds, whom we think we can control. Because we have failed to appreciate God's revelation through beautiful singing, friendly dialogue with God, and beautiful flowers, we have created artificial and unnatural ideas about beauty that are dehumanizing and destructive.

In the Nahuatl text (v. 19), Juan Diego hears Our Lady's thought and her word, which he finds to be "exceedingly re-creative, very ennobling, alluring, producing love." This is a perfect description of the effects that the word of God brings about in the person who hears and receives it. In our response to the word of God, we are totally re-created into new being. This is salvation. The old, defeated, victimized, "inferior," humiliated, "worthless" self ceases to exist, and a new, confident, noble, self-assured, joyful human person arises. Through faith, we are totally rehabilitated in our humanity as men and women. This new person will have no need of becoming like the victimizing conquistador (the ongoing curse of the creole and mestizo) but will be him/herself in a radically new way. This is redemptive birth. This is the beginning of the truly "new church" of the eventual new humanity of the New World, which was just beginning to dawn at Tepeyac.... This new person does not have to copy anyone but is able to respond freely to God's invitation.

True faith is always ennobling, for we become conscious that as children of God, we are not inferior to anyone else. Faith rehabilitates us in our original dignity as creatures made in the image and likeness of God and therefore affirms us as creatures of unquestioned beauty and infinite dignity and worth. Like the grace of the Visitation, which enabled Mary to rejoice in the unique conception of her child even though others did not understand it and even rejected it with scorn (e.g., Joseph thought of divorce), the grace of Our Lady's thought and word ennobles those who experience them, even though they are surrounded by rejection and domination. They are strengthened and empowered through their newfound sense of inner dignity and human worth.

The grace and allurement Our Lady offers also parallel those offered by Jesus. Jesus attracted the poor, the hopeless, and the marginated of his time not by criticizing them, by belittling their religious practices, or by threatening them with hell. Jesus brought good news to the poor, sight to the blind, and liberty to the captives. That is why he was so attractive to the masses of damned humanity and so repulsive to the religiously correct people of his time. Guadalupe is just like that. And to the *massa damnata,* Our Lady continues to be alluring, calling all the hurting, disfigured, and disinherited to herself. It is like the call of Jesus: "Come to me all of you who are tired and weary, and I will refresh you." Her gentleness, evident concern, and compassionate love are the source of her re-creating power.

When faith re-creates us, making us God's children in the image and likeness of God, it makes us loving, since God is love. It is by this unlimited love now alive in us through the power of the Spirit that others will know we are truly God's disciples. If evangelization does not begin with this love within the missionary and eventually produce this love in the person who responds in faith, it has failed. All true evangelization is about love. Doctrines, dogmas, and ethical codes will certainly follow, but without living and burning love, they are nothing but the deadening noise of pieces of metal clanging together.

It Is about God

The most fascinating aspect of Guadalupe is that it introduces us to a more comprehensive and open-ended concept of God — a mestizo God. In Our Lady, the Spanish and the Nahuatl concepts of God are beautifully combined to present us with an understanding of God that is fuller than either one of them had suspected. Guadalupe purifies both notions of God, takes nothing away from their original manifestation, and enriches both. But Our Lady does not present two gods. There is only one God who is known in various ways, and Our Lady is the mother of that God. She stimulates new ways to think about God — for instance, she challenged the patriarchal Christianity of that time with the reality of the femininity of God.

The opening texts state that we are at the very beginning of the new era of faith in God:

Thus faith started; it gave its first buds; and it flowered in the knowledge of the One through Whom We Live, the true God, Téotl. (v. 4)

The whole text of Guadalupe is about the beginning of faith in the one true God. But this opening is very illuminative, for it is a highly interreligious and inclusive text that opens the way for a new understanding of God that goes beyond the Nahuatl and the Spanish notions of God. It will embody both but go beyond both by producing something new. The absolute religious claims of various peoples function as an ultimate barrier that can even sacralize segregation and justify hate. Recognizing this, Guadalupe respects the two apparently irreconcilable religious views, takes in what is good in both of them, avoids what is false in both, and offers a new synthesis that will bring together the true aspects of both through a new imagery of God.

By uniting "the One through Whom We Live" with the "true God, Téotl," the narrative has united the Nahuatl concept of God, which was abominable to the Spaniards, with the Spanish concept of God, which was incomprehensible to the Indians. Both become interpretive of each other. The interreligious conversion that the missioners had abhorred is now initiated and established as normative for the new church of the Americas. The Christian God of the missioners begins to be incarnated — enfleshed — in the imagery of God of the ancient traditions of pre-Columbian America.[8] She opens the way for the deepest and most humanizing dialogue, for the way we conceive of God is the way we ultimately conceive of ourselves. The way we see God is ultimately the way we see ourselves, and only a true image of God can give us a true image of who we truly are as human beings. In Our Lady, the opposition between the two humanities based on the two contradictory religions is converted into harmony, and the ultimate source of division is eliminated. As our notions of God can be combined so that we might appreciate God all the more, so must our notions of humanity be shared and combined (not one eliminating the other) for the sake of a better and greater humanity. This is true human progress.

This new synthesis is further elaborated when the Lady introduces herself to Juan:

> *"I am the Ever-Virgin Holy Mary, Mother of the God of Great Truth, Téotl, of the One through Whom We Live, the Creator of Persons, the Owner of What Is Near and Together, of the Lord of Heaven and Earth."* (v. 22)

This is an astounding sentence. The missioners were trying to discredit and destroy the Indian gods. Foreign missioners to this day are afraid of the religious ideas of natives, and Euro-American Christianity is still suspicious of any type of syncretism, forgetting the creative syncretism of its own Euro-Christian origins. Our Lady of Guadalupe is beyond this ethnocentric fear and introduces herself as the mother of a multidimensional God. The images Our Lady offers may not present a complete picture of God, but they are definitely not false or diabolical. The God of Great Truth has philosophical characteristics and speaks to us about the truth of God; the One through Whom We Live is centered upon humanity and the lives of men and women; the Creator of Persons is much

---

8. Clodomiro L. Siller Acuña, *Para comprender el mensaje de María de Guadalupe* (Buenos Aires: Editorial Guadalupe, 1989), 59.

more than the impersonal Creator of heaven and earth — God is the creator of our personality; the Lord of What Is Near and Together is the unifying center of all our existence: within ourselves and with other persons, animals, nature, and the cosmos. God is the ground, center, and highest aspiration of all being. God is the root of our culture, the core of our cultural unity, and the highest aspiration of our culture.

By using the names of the Gods of the ancient Nahuatl pantheon,[9] Our Lady is affirming that she is their mother too. (Her litany of names is in some ways equivalent to saying, "the God of Abraham, Isaac, Jacob, Moses, David, and Jesus.") She is the mother of their ancestors, who are thus to be revered and venerated, as it was through them that they had been advancing in their pilgrimage of faith. Furthermore, to balance the emphasis on the fatherhood of God, she emphasizes the motherhood of God — after all, only a Father-Mother God could adequately image the origins of all life. The one-sided emphasis of the missioners is thus corrected and enhanced by the Virgin Mother of God. The male Father God of militaristic and patriarchal Christianity is united to the female Mother God (Tonantzin), which allows the original heart and face of Christianity to shine forth: compassion, understanding, tenderness, and healing. The harsh and punishing "God of judgment" of the West is tempered with the listening and healing "companion," while the all-powerful conquering God is transformed into a loving and caring Parent. The distant God of dogmatic formula and abstraction is dissolved into a friendly and intimate presence. At the same time, the distant, faceless, and complicated gods of the Nahuatls are assumed into the very human though divine person of Our Lady of Guadalupe.

Just as Guadalupe corrects the Spanish concept of God, so she corrects the Indian conceptualization of God. The blood-thirsty gods who demanded human sacrifice are not mentioned as her children. She mentions only the names of the gods for whom there was no imagery and who belonged to the purest theology of an-

---

9. In their pilgrimage to Tenochtitlán, as they captured various nations, the Nahuatl had incorporated the conquered people's gods into their own pantheon. Thus their pantheon includes many former deities of the various nations of Mexico.

cient times. As mentioned earlier, these are the same names that the *tlamatini* (wise men/theologians) mentioned to the missioners in the famous dialogues with the twelve "apostles" (first Franciscan missioners) and that the missioners found abominable and totally antagonistic to their own "one, true God." Guadalupe assumes them in the same plane of veracity and dignity as the God of the missioners. Thus she corrects the Spanish misunderstanding and rectifies the insults (blasphemies to the natives) of the missioners.[10] But she also inserts the God of the missioners into the religious tradition of the ancient Mexicans — paralleling, in some ways, what Paul did with the Greeks and the early church fathers did with the great philosophical traditions of Greece. They inserted the trinitarian God of Jesus into previous traditions so that the people could understand and accept Jesus.

Guadalupe brings about what even the best and most sensitive missioners would not have wanted or even suspected as salutary: the mutually enriching dialogue of the Christian notions of God with the Nahuatl notions of God. In this Guadalupan synthesis, the good news of new life breaks through. This is not a juxtaposition or a coexistence of opposing notions of God but the real *birth* of something new. The two religions need not kill one another and should come together as in the conjugal relation to produce a new offspring — in continuity with both yet transformative of both into something new. This new creation receives life from both but is not a mere extension or simple continuity of either. It is a new child, a new humanity, a new church. Both had so much to offer to each other, but neither could see it or even think about it. God breaks through — with flower and song! This is no longer an exterminator God, but is, rather, the God of pleasure and harmony.

This new mestizo understanding of God is not a restricted and closed notion that will justify opposition between peoples; rather, it is an open notion that will allow for growth and expansion and a gradual appreciation of the infinite that is ultimately beyond our best understanding and formulation.[11] This will be made possible

---

10. Siller Acuña, *Para comprender el mensaje*, 68.
11. In many ways, I think this is what Archbishop John Quinn was referring to

in the Americas through the Nahuatl (indigenous) Mother religion and the Christian Father religion, producing a proud child who will come from both and go beyond both unto something new! This is the Christ child carried in the womb of the Indian Mother of the Americas.

It Is about Christ and the New Humanity

The redemption of the New World begins at Tepeyac. At the very center of the Guadalupe image is the Nahuatl glyph that appears at the center of the old Aztec representation of the cosmos, commonly referred to as the Aztec calendar. This indicates that the previous ages — "Suns" — of the world have been assumed and a new one is about to begin. If there had been five previous Suns, she is now the beginning of the Sixth Sun. The glyph is immediately over her womb, and the black band over her waist indicates she is pregnant, as is also evident in her puffed cheeks. She carries within her the new source and center of the humanity of the final age. As in the incarnation God chose to begin through the cooperation of a woman, so now, too, the coming together of the entire planet for the first time will begin with a woman.

Juan Diego recognizes this when he tells the bishop that La Virgen is the mother of our Lord and Savior Jesus Christ. La Virgen never told him this, but he deduced this from what he heard from her, what he saw in her, and what he had heard from the missioners about the Savior. This, as argued earlier, is the beginning of true Christian theological reflection in the New World. The innermost core of the apparition, even though La Virgen never mentions it as such, is what she carries within her womb: the new source and center of the new humanity that is about to be born. And that source and center is Christ as the light and life of the world.

---

at a major conference at Oxford, England, in the summer of 1996. Quinn called for major changes in our present-day ecclesial and theological structures for the sake of a greater human and religious unity — relativizing even the most sacred traditions for the sake of the sacredness of God.

The image is both the sign and the announcement of the truly new creation of the Americas — not a "new" world that would simply rebuild the old ways of conquest, greed, avarice, subjugation, and wars in a new space, but a new world that would be authentically new because of its inclusion of all the peoples of all the Americas as children of the one Mother. This image offers a condemnation of the "Christian" societies of the New World that would be based on racial segregation, classism, racism, sexism, enslavement, and exploitation. In asking for a temple where she can give all her love and compassion, the Lady is in effect speaking about the reign of God that was the core of the life and message of Jesus. Guadalupe is thus a good Nahuatl translation of the New Testament reality of the reign of God as revealed by Jesus. Our Lady is calling for a new temple that will be sacred precisely because segregation and discrimination will have no place there. The unity of all peoples will make it sacred, and that is what her presence as loving and compassionate Mother wants to bring about. If she is the one who attracts, it is through the power of her Son that this will come about. The mother-son relation is as evident and crucial to the whole message as the mother-son relation in the Gospels' descriptions of the wedding feast at Cana.

It Is about the Triune God

The doctrine of the triune God, which is rooted in the best of anthropological imagery, is one of the great achievements of Christian theological reflection. That reflection is not, however, complete or closed. The image of the triune God develops as each of us reflects on it. I experienced something of this while visiting the basilica at Tepeyac and conversing with Our Lady eye to eye on the morning of September 14, 1995. There were thousands of pilgrims there, but it seemed she was there, personally, for each one of us. She and I had a conversation about many things. All of a sudden a thought was so obvious and as real as her apparition must have been for Juan Diego: the Indian Mother sends her Christian-Indian child to call the Christian father-bishop to become a home-builder. For me, this flash was like a new picture of the triune God presented in the imagery of the New World. This New World imagery of the Trinity has fascinating implications and is pregnant with theological and anthropological possibilities — some of which I have tried to explore in this work.

The Old World had expressed its knowledge of the triune God through the imagery and language of its patriarchal worldview. Yet we know that because God is infinite, the fullness of our knowledge and understanding of God is ahead of us and is slowly developing through time. Through the Guadalupan trinitarian imagery, the New World makes a major contribution to the

> growth in the understanding of the realities and the words which have been handed down. This happens through the contemplation and study made by believers, who treasure these things in their hearts (cf. Lk 2:19, 51), through the intimate understanding of spiritual things they experience, and through the preaching of those who have received through episcopal succession the sure gift of truth. (*Dei Verbum*, no. 8)[12]

This authentically American contribution to the understanding of Christian faith can illuminate in a new way the central doctrine[13] of our faith, the mystery of the Most Holy Trinity, and thus make its unique contribution to the entire church.[14] Our Lady of Guadalupe does not suggest a new doctrine. Rather, she offers alternative basic imagery for this doctrine so that it might be better understood, appreciated, and loved. Perhaps this is her greatest gift to the universal fellowship of Christians: she illumines the indwelling of the Blessed Trinity — the mystery of God — through

---

12. For a presentation of the preaching on the theological signification of Our Lady of Guadalupe, see F. Schulte, *A Mexican Spirituality of Divine Election for Mission: Its Sources in the Unpublished Sermons, 1661–1821* (Rome: Pontifical Gregorian University, 1994); see also the pontifical declarations on Our Lady of Guadalupe, especially those of John Paul II.

13. *The Catechism of the Catholic Church*, no. 234.

14. Nebel, *Santa María Tonantzin*, 294.

the image of the Mother who sends the child to call the Father so that together they may create a new home for everyone.

God will be fully revealed in the Americas when the harmony of Mother-children-Father comes about and there is an end to abused women, abandoned children, and runaway fathers; when there is an end to patriarchal/hierarchical societies that put some down while elevating others to positions of power and prestige; when there is an end to the various structures of the Americas that keep people apart or excluded. The new temple that houses the new humanity of the Americas must begin in the home — that is where Juan Bernardino was healed — and extend to the whole of the Americas. This will be a humanity that reflects and images the likeness of the triune God — Mother-child-Father. In the name of the Mother who sends the child to call the Father to build a home for all, a new humanity has been born, and a new appreciation of the mystery of God has been initiated.

Closing Thoughts

I can think of no better way of closing these reflections than by quoting a great Old World (German) theologian and Guadalupe scholar, Richard Nebel:

> The theological language and content of the *Nican Mopohua*, based on the message of Our Lady of Guadalupe, are determined by the vision of a harmonious equilibrium, an equilibrium of solidarity and fraternity which are contained in the new Cosmic Order.[15]

My conviction, which I have tried to reflect throughout these pages, is that this new cosmic order started with the Guadalupe event. It is just beginning, and in time it will come to plenitude. It is, however, a difficult process because the profound anthropological and theological implications of Guadalupe have been kept

---

15. Nebel, *Santa María Tonantzin,* 262.

hidden by relegating Our Lady to the sphere of the popular devotion of the uninformed masses of Mexican Catholics. The sermons of the 1600s and 1700s were a good beginning at getting at the meaning of Guadalupe, but we must go much further because "the body of the faithful as a whole, anointed as they are by the Holy One (cf. John 2:20, 27), cannot err in matters of belief" (*Lumen Gentium,* no. 12). The church of the Americas must continue the creative and critical reflection on the full meaning and implications of this constant and growing belief of the faithful. The debate about the historicity of the event, like that on the historical Jesus, is long-standing, yet the theological reflection based on the unquestioned reality of her living presence in the faithful, as the Risen Lord is present in the faithful, is just beginning, and I have no doubt it will lead us to exciting discoveries as the church of the Americas develops the particularity of its New World tradition.

Our Lady of Guadalupe is about the liberation of the gospel so that it might appear in all its salvific grandeur to the peoples who were encountering it for the first time and, even more so, to the people who thought they already had it. To appreciate the true meaning, depth, and extent of Guadalupe we must not only situate it in the historical context of the violent and unequal encounter of two worlds but also allow ourselves to go beyond the limitations of our anthropologies and attempt to see, hear, and understand it through a mestizo anthropology — an anthropology of inclusive and progressive synthesis.

At that unique moment in the history of our planet, God intervened to open up the possibilities for the eventual unity of all peoples. Human beings wanted to conquer, divide, and dominate — spiritually and/or physically — but God wanted to convert, unite, liberate, and create a common home for everyone. We — Europeans and natives — wanted bloodshed and victims, but God wanted flower and songs. We wanted battles, forced labor, and the whip, but God wanted fiesta, compassion, and love. Guadalupe, like Jesus, reverses the intent and purpose of the world by introducing a totally new creation, a totally new vision of the new humanity, a totally new way of bringing it about, a new cosmic order. She opens the way for a global universality that the

world has never known: a universality of harmony, a universality of respect for others in their differences, a universality of appreciation of differences, a universality of love, compassion, and mutual aid. This is the ultimate cosmic order that we need to work to bring about.

John the Apostle had a vision, which I cited earlier, of this type of newness breaking forth:

> And a great sign appeared in heaven:
> a woman clothed with the sun
> and the moon under her feet
> and upon her head, a crown of twelve stars.
> And being with child,
> she cried out in her travail
> and was in the anguish of delivery. (Rev. 12:1–2)

The conquest was killing off Our Lady's children. The new world order would soon seek to destroy all differences or enslave and exploit the weaker other. The mother of the new world order does not want this. She cries out to let her children be born and demands a caring and loving home for all the children of this earth.

Our Lady of Guadalupe is not just another Marian apparition. Guadalupe has to do with the very core of the gospel itself. It is nothing less than an original American Gospel, a narrative of a birth/resurrection experience at the very beginning of the crucifixion of the natives, the Africans, and their mestizo and mulatto children. The condemned and crucified peoples of the Americas were homeless, alone, and without protection. But God would triumph. The final and greatest gift of our Virgin Mother was her miraculous painting in the *tilma* of Juan Diego, which was given first to the bishop and then to all of us. Her gift of that image — a living gift that would keep her memory alive among the people — was like Jesus' gift of the Spirit. La Virgen wanted to stay with us for all time, reminding us of her life-giving message, and she does so through her sacred icon.

The image on the *tilma* is not just a painting. It is a recapitulation of the message that Juan Diego experienced, saw, and heard at Tepeyac. In the native cloth of Juan Diego's *tilma* — the fiber of the clothing of the poorest of the poor of the conquered and dominated people — the image of the unlimited and very personal love and compassion of the new center of all life and of the universe made its dwelling among us. Like the biblical word that was written on paper made by human hands in a specific place, God's word was painted on the native cloth of indigenous America. Like the biblical word, it would be there for all generations to "read" for our salvation. What the written word has been for generations of biblical believers, the painted word has been for generations of believers in the New World. In Our Lady of Guadalupe at Tepeyac, God pitched a tent and came to dwell among us. The Word became flesh of the Americas through Our Lady of Guadalupe and dwells among us truly as one of us.

Her icon is her living presence looking at us and speaking with us as she did with Juan Diego. In her eyes, we find recognition, acceptance, respect, and confidence. She is always present in the Tepeyacs of the world — the barrios, the slums, the public housing projects, the ghettos, and other such places. She will never leave us because she has been intimately woven into the cloth of our suffering-resurrecting existence. While others crucify us, she resurrects us.

Guadalupe is the most prodigious event since the coming of our Lord and Savior, Jesus Christ. Her compassionate *rostro y corazón* (countenance and heart) are alive not only on the *tilma* of Juan Diego but also in the faces and hearts of all who see her, call upon her, and believe in her. She is here among us where and when we need her; she is always present to rehabilitate the broken, uplift the downtrodden, console the afflicted, accompany the lonely, and give life to the dying. She has been a source of energy and inspiration for many who have struggled for liberty and justice in the Americas: for Father Miguel Hidalgo, César Chávez, Dolores Huerta, Adelita Navarro, Samuel Ruiz, and for many others who have found their heroic strength for survival within her. She continues to be what she said she was: the merciful Mother who is with us to give us all her love, compassion, help, and protection — to hear our laments and remedy and cure all the miseries, pains, and sorrows.

She is truly the gospel of life in the new human fiber of the Americas. Her project is just beginning, but it is indeed underway. We must collaborate with her call to work together to bring it about — a common home for all the inhabitants of the Americas and the world.

Bibliography

Aquino, María Pilar. *Our Cry for Life: A Feminist Theology from Latin America*. Maryknoll, N.Y.: Orbis Books, 1993.

Boff, Leonardo, and Virgil Elizondo, eds. *1492–1992: The Voice of the Victims*. Vol. 1990/6 of *Concilium*. London: SCM Press, 1990.

Borobio, Dionisio, ed. *La primera evangelización de América*. Salamanca: Universidad Pontificia de Salamanca, 1992.

Cervantes, Fernando. *The Devil in the New World*. New Haven: Yale University Press, 1994.

Chauvet, Fidel de Jesús. *El culto guadalupano del Tepeyac*. Mexico City: Centro de Estudios Bernardino de Sahagún, 1978.

Cox, Harvey. *Fire from Heaven*. New York: Free Press, 1995.

de la Torre Villar, Ernesto, and Ramiro Navarro de Anda. *Testimonios históricos guadalupanos*. Mexico City: Fondo de Cultura Económica, 1982.

Elizondo, Virgil. *The Future Is Mestizo: Life Where Cultures Meet*. New York: Crossroad, 1988.

———. *Galilean Journey: The Mexican-American Promise*. Maryknoll, N.Y.: Orbis Books, 1983.

———. *La Morenita: Evangelizer of the Americas*. San Antonio: Mexican American Cultural Center, 1981.

———. *Way of the Cross: Passion of Christ in the Americas*. Maryknoll, N.Y.: Orbis Books, 1992.

Espín, Orlando. "Grace and Humanness." In *We Are a People*, ed. Roberto Goizueta. Philadelphia: Fortress Press, 1992.

———. "Trinitarian Monotheism and the Birth of Popular Catholicism: The Case of Sixteenth-Century Mexico." *Missiology* 20, no. 2 (1992).

Floristán, Casiano, "Evangelization of the 'New World': An Old World Perspective," *Missiology* 20, no. 2 (1992).

Fragoso Castanares, Alberto. "Vida del Beato Juan Diego." *Histórica: Organo del Centro de Estudios Guadalupanos* 2 (June 1991).

García-Rivera, Alejandro. *St. Martin de Porres: The "Little Stories" and the Semiotics of Culture*. Maryknoll, N.Y.: Orbis Books, 1995.

Goizueta, Roberto. *Caminemos con Jesús: Toward a Hispanic/Latino Theology of Accompaniment.* Maryknoll, N.Y.: Orbis Books, 1995.

González, Justo. "Voices of Compassion." *Missiology* 20, no. 2 (1992).

Goodpasture, H. McKennie. *Cross and Sword: An Eyewitness History of Christianity in Latin America.* Maryknoll, N.Y.: Orbis Books, 1989.

Gruzinski, Serge. *The Conquest of Mexico.* New York: Polity Press, 1993.

———. *La guerre des images.* Paris: Fayard, 1990.

Küng, Hans. *The Council, Reform and Reunion.* New York: Sheed and Ward, 1961.

Lafaye, Jacques. *Quetzalcoatl and Guadalupe.* Chicago: University of Chicago Press, 1976.

Le Clezio, J. M. G. *The Mexican Dream: The Interrupted Thought of Amerindian Civilizations.* Chicago: University of Chicago Press, 1993.

León-Portilla, Miguel. *Aztec Thought and Culture.* Norman: University of Oklahoma Press, 1963.

———. *Endangered Cultures.* Dallas: Southern Methodist University Press, 1990.

———. *Visión de los vencidos.* Mexico City: UNAM, 1972.

Maravall, José Antonio. *El mundo social de "La Celestina."* Madrid: Editorial Gredos, 1972.

Mauricio y Jiménez, Gabriel. "La santa imagen del Tepeyac: Lo que ahí está y no hemos visto." *Histórica: Organo del Centro de Estudios Guadalupanos* 1 (March 1991).

Morner, Magnus. *Race Mixture in Latin America.* Boston: Little, Brown and Co., 1967.

Nebel, Richard. *Santa María Tonantzin: Virgen de Guadalupe.* Mexico City: Fondo de Cultura Económica, 1995.

Pallares, Salvador. "La aparición de la Virgen de Guadalupe," *Servir* 17, nos. 93–94 (1981)

Paz, Octavio. *The Labyrinth of Solitude.* New York: Grove Press, 1961.

Pineda, Ana María, "Evangelization of the 'New World': A New World Perspective." *Missiology* 20, no. 2 (1992).

Ribiero, Darcy. "The Latin American People." In *1492–1992: The Voice of the Victims,* ed. Leonardo Boff and Virgil Elizondo. Vol. 1990/6 of *Concilium.* London: SCM Press, 1990.

Ricard, Robert. *The Spiritual Conquest of Mexico: The Evangelizing Methods of the Mendicant Orders in New Spain, 1523–1572.* Reprint. Berkeley: University of California Press, 1966 [1933].

Rivera Herrera, Hugo D. *Presencia de Santa María de Guadalupe en el pueblo mexicano.* Mexico City: Editorial Progreso, 1994.

Rivera Pagán, Luis N. "Conquest and Colonization: The Problem of America." *Apuntes* 12, no. 2 (1992).

———. *A Violent Evangelization.* Louisville: Westminster/John Knox Press, 1992.

Rodríguez, Jeanette. *Our Lady of Guadalupe: Faith and Empowerment among Mexican-American Women.* Austin: University of Texas Press, 1993.

Salinas, Carlos, and Manuel de la Mora. *Descubrimiento de un busto humano en los ojos de la Virgen de Guadalupe.* Mexico City: Editorial Tradición, 1980.

Schulte, F. *A Mexican Spirituality of Divine Election for Mission: Its Sources in the Unpublished Sermons, 1661–1821.* Rome: Pontifical Gregorian University, 1994.

Sierra, Justo. *The Political Evolution of the Mexican People.* Austin: University of Texas Press, 1969.

Siller Acuña, Clodomiro L. "El método de evangelización en el Nican Mopohua." *Servir* 17, nos. 93–94 (1981).

———. *Para comprender el mensaje de María de Guadalupe.* Buenos Aires: Editorial Guadalupe, 1989.

———. "Para una teología del Nican Mopohua." *Servir* 12, no. 62 (1976).

Smith, Jody. *The Image of Guadalupe: Myth or Miracle?* New York: Doubleday, 1984.

Sylvest, Ed. *Motifs of Franciscan Missionary Spirit in New Spain.* Washington, D.C.: Academy of American Franciscan History, 1975.

———. *Nuestra Señora de Guadalupe, Mother of God.* Dallas: Southern Methodist University Press, 1992.

Tinker, George. *Missionary Conquest: The Gospel and Native American Cultural Genocide.* Minneapolis: Fortress Press, 1993.